D0395415

DISCARD

Get a Life, Not a Job

Art Center College Library
1700 Lida Street
Pasadena, CA 91103

ART CENTER COLLEGE OF DESIGN

3 3220 00295 2096

650.1
C153
2010

DISCARD

Get a Life, Not a Job

Do What You Love and Let Your Talents Work For You

Art Center College Library
1700 Lida Street
Pasadena, CA 91103

Paula Caligiuri, Ph.D.

Vice President, Publisher: Tim Moore
Associate Publisher and Director of Marketing: Amy Neidlinger
Acquisitions Editor: Jennifer Simon
Editorial Assistant: Myesha Graham
Development Editor: Russ Hall
Operations Manager: Gina Kanouse
Senior Marketing Manager: Julie Phifer
Publicity Manager: Laura Czaja
Assistant Marketing Manager: Megan Colvin
Cover Designer: Alan Clements
Managing Editor: Kristy Hart
Project Editor: Betsy Harris
Copy Editor: Karen Annett
Proofreader: Dan Knott
Senior Indexer: Cheryl Lenser
Compositor: Jake McFarland
Manufacturing Buyer: Dan Uhrig

© 2010 by Pearson Education, Inc.
Publishing as FT Press
Upper Saddle River, New Jersey 07458

FT Press offers excellent discounts on this book when ordered in quantity for bulk purchases or special sales. For more information, please contact U.S. Corporate and Government Sales, 1-800-382-3419, corpsales@pearsontechgroup.com. For sales outside the U.S., please contact International Sales at international@pearson.com.

Company and product names mentioned herein are the trademarks or registered trademarks of their respective owners.

All rights reserved. No part of this book may be reproduced, in any form or by any means, without permission in writing from the publisher.

Printed in the United States of America

First Printing March 2010 with corrections August 2011

This product is printed digitally on demand.

ISBN-10: 0-13-705849-7
ISBN-13: 978-0-13-705849-5

Pearson Education LTD.
Pearson Education Australia PTY, Limited.
Pearson Education Singapore, Pte. Ltd.
Pearson Education North Asia, Ltd.
Pearson Education Canada, Ltd.
Pearson Educación de Mexico, S.A. de C.V.
Pearson Education—Japan
Pearson Education Malaysia, Pte. Ltd.

Library of Congress Cataloging-in-Publication Data
Caligiuri, Paula.
   Get a life, not a job : do what you love and let your talents work for you / Paula Caligiuri.
      p. cm. Includes bibliographical references.
   ISBN-13: 978-0-13-705849-5 (pbk. : alk. paper)
   ISBN-10: 0-13-705849-7 (pbk. : alk. paper) 1. Vocational guidance. 2. Career development. I. Title.
   HF5381.C25316 2010
   650.1—dc22

                              2009051715

*To Judy, Harvey, and Rick for sage guidance
and unconditional love over many years*

Contents

Acknowledgments

Every book, including *Get a Life, Not a Job,* has its own life story. This book was conceived from conversations with those willing to talk to me about their jobs, from those I love the most in the world, my siblings and best friends, to those stuck in airline clubs during long layovers, whose names I might have forgotten but whose stories have remained with me. I thank them for their honesty and openness.

Get a Life, Not a Job ultimately took shape last year when the downsizing bully started messing with people I love. It broke my heart to see the emotional toll that unfulfilling jobs and corporate layoffs were taking on highly talented and hardworking individuals. Believing they deserved more—a lot more—in return for their efforts, I started to write.

Get a Life, Not a Job has a soul thanks to those profiled in this book. Their willingness to share their career stories has made the advice in this book real and has demonstrated that career fulfillment is abundantly attainable. Without your stories, this book would not be possible. You are each worthy of deep admiration; you each have remained true to your personal values, defining and achieving career success on your terms. You have my sincerest appreciation.

Although not as theoretically rich as this profession deserves, *Get a Life, Not a Job*'s backbone is rooted in my academic discipline, industrial and organizational psychology (SIOP, Division 14 of the American Psychological Association), and the many talented practitioners and researchers who continually advance our knowledge of how people interact with the work they do. I realize I only skimmed the surface of what our profession has to offer the world of work. I wish there was space on the pages to cite the many amazing researchers who have built this profession and the knowledge base creating the field. This book offers a very small piece of a theoretically rich academic field. I thank my academic colleagues who knew I was writing this book and encouraged me to do so, even though the style led me away from my academic comfort zone.

I thank the many people who have read versions of *Get a Life, Not a Job* offering their critical feedback and keen insights, Beth Atwood, Daniel Fennell, Dan Frontera, Sue Frontera, Gabrielle D'Annunzio, Leah Lewandowski, Ted Munger, and Elsa Peterson. The book is a better product as a result of their contributions. I thank my siblings, John and Linda Caligiuri, Terry and Joe Gentile, and Tom and Jenny Caligiuri, and my parents, Angie and John Caligiuri, for offering support (and more than a little comic relief) throughout the writing process.

My gratitude is extended to my agent Joe Veltre for taking a chance on an unknown and for saying the most satisfying words to an author's ears: *"I'd like to send a copy of your book to my friend."* In thanking Joe, I also need to thank those who brought me to him: Bob Sutton, Don Lamm, and Christy Fletcher. They were generous with their time and contacts, realizing I was an academic very lost in a different type of publishing world.

My heartfelt appreciation is also extended to my senior editor from FT Press, Jennifer Simon. Jennifer knew, as an academic, I was a fish out of water. I am very grateful for her advice, honesty, and sensitivity in helping me make this transition. Writing this book has given me the opportunity to cross paths with wonderful people, including Nadia Bilchik, Grayson Leverenz, Mary Pomerantz, and Tom Severini. I deeply appreciate their gifts of time, creativity, support, and friendship—they have been generous with all of them.

I have been blessed in life to have a muse, my husband George D'Annunzio. He has cleared the decks for me on many days so I could be alone with my computer and my thoughts. He has patiently read countless drafts of this book. George instinctively knew when to give me space and when I needed breaks, accommodating both so well, as only a loving muse can. I love and appreciate George for many reasons, not the least of which is his willingness to join me in crafting my own life story, as I create my own career acts.

This book is dedicated to Judy Larkin, Harvey Pines, and Rick Jacobs, my outstanding mentors and dear friends. For over 20 years, they have been helping me discover my strengths, explore my interests, and find the career acts best suited to me. Their love for me is evidenced by their unwavering support, encouragement, and steadfast belief in what I could become, regardless of how much time it took for them to find my talents, shape my skills, and polish my abilities. Their love is also evidenced by the countless times they would not let me off the hook, asking me those tough questions, leading me to uncover the truth about myself. You know you are deeply loved when someone takes the time to walk with you in your road to self-discovery. I would not be who I am or what I am today without the love of Judy, Harvey, and Rick—and my love for them runs deeper than I will ever have the words to fully express.

About the Author

Paula Caligiuri, Ph.D., is a Professor in the Human Resource Management Department at Rutgers University where she directed the Center for HR Strategy from 2001 through 2010. She has been recognized as one of the most prolific authors in the field of international business for her work in global careers and global leadership development. Paula has written (with Steven Poelmans) *Harmonizing Work, Family, and Personal Life* (Cambridge Press, 2008) and (with Dave Lepak and Jaime Bonache) *Managing the Global Workforce* (Wiley, 2010). She has covered career-related topics for CNN and has hosted a pilot for a television show, *CareerWATCH*. Paula holds a Ph.D. from Penn State University in industrial and organizational psychology.

introduction

The way to achieve career success has changed so dramatically in recent years that much of the advice offered in schools, companies, and even homes—by well-meaning counselors, managers, parents, spouses, and friends—is outdated. *Get a Life, Not a Job* offers you a new approach to your relationship with work, a way to invest in and grow your career in a way that will enable you to achieve financial security while freeing yourself from any one employer that, frankly, might not have a job for you tomorrow.

Although some elements in the formula for career success have endured, such as conscientiousness, reliability, performance excellence, and possession of valuable skills, many of the elements for career success have, indeed, changed. *Get a Life, Not a Job* is based on the new employment reality and the real dynamics of today's world of work.

Get a Life, Not a Job is a guide to designing your life that includes your career—expanding and creating new career-related activities *purposefully* to do more of what you enjoy and in the way you want to engage with your career. It shows you how to find multiple income-creating and wealth-producing activities that offer you more excitement, fulfillment, and security. The approach offers you tremendous personal and financial freedom because you are not relying on one source of income and your destiny is not tied to that of your employer's.

What do *you* call income-creating activities that are stimulating, desirable, enjoyable, balanced, dynamic, exciting, financially rewarding, and liberating—other than a "winning lottery ticket," a "large trust fund," or a "delusion"? I call them **career acts. Career acts** are simultaneous and stimulating profitable activities composed of what people (who enjoy what they do) engage in for a living.

Why *Now* Is the Best Time to Get a Life, Not a Job

I wrote this book because too many people today are unhappy with their employment situation, unsure of what to do after college, currently unemployed, or disillusioned by their career or the occupation they selected. In today's employment reality, employees are less able to predict their professional futures than ever before—and this lack of predictability and uncertainty has been causing unprecedented levels of stress among employees. *Would it surprise you that in a recent survey of Americans, almost 80% of the recently unemployed received less than three weeks in advance warning—among them,* **60% received no advance warning that they were to be unemployed?**[1] Yikes!

As almost everyone who is currently working knows, this "career plan" or *psychological contract* with employers is obsolete and largely a fool's mission for those who still expect it with most firms in today's employment reality. Dr. Denise Rousseau, a leader in research on the psychological contract, defines it as *an individual's belief in mutual obligations between that person and another party, such as an employer.*[2] Over the course of the past couple of decades, the psychological contract between employers and employees has clearly changed in one important way: Employers have no long-term commitment to their employees and employees have no long-term commitment to their employers. Employers provide income and benefits in return for employees' high performance. There are no guarantees that there will be a job in the future, just as there is no expectation that you will stay with the organization if there is a better opportunity for you elsewhere. It's understandable that some American employees might be nostalgic for the old psychological contract that seemed to offer long-term financial security, stability, and benefits. But, frankly, there is no evidence that it will ever return.

2

Compared with employees, it seems that employers are far more comfortable with today's new psychological contract. Employers can now leverage a variety of cost-effective employment configurations, including the hiring of part-time employees, independent contractors, and contingent workers—and the moving of manufacturing, semi-skilled, and professional jobs to countries where labor costs are low. These new employment configurations have helped firms become more competitive in today's global economy by offering employers financial flexibility in their wage bills. However, what might be good for corporate bottom lines might not be the best thing for employees' careers.

Please don't misunderstand me: I am *not* against business. There are, in fact, many fine organizations out there that are finding it tougher to compete globally and need to use a greater variety of lower-cost employment configurations to remain competitive.[3] Companies understand and leverage the new psychological contract because of the competitive pressures they face. On the other hand, employees, for the most part, do not fully comprehend the speed at which the contract has changed and is continuing to change. To level the playing field, *Get a Life, Not a Job* highlights these changes; I want you to fully understand the new employment reality so you can effectively navigate it. Above all, I want you to own your own career destiny because that is what this new psychological contract demands.

What is generally understood about the current psychological contract? Employees have grown comfortable with the idea of changing employers, but many still seek full-time positions with consecutive organizations. Rather than commitment to any one organization, we have convinced ourselves that by "staying marketable," we will be desired (and hopefully courted) by future employers. We are, in many ways, trying to re-create the old psychological contract in a serial sense, across successive employers (that is, *if I perform well in my field, I'll be employed long-term*). Part of this statement is true, but only if you possess the most highly sought-out skills.

If you are working, and are like most people, you spend time while in your current job thinking about your next job. But, unfortunately, the macro psychological contract that underlies the logic of employability across sequential employers exists only for a small percentage of people in key positions or occupations within certain industries. For most, you are not in control of your career because maintaining predictable marketability in a dynamic employment system is very difficult. This is the new reality.

I propose that we break this cycle: Rather than a preoccupation with whether you'll have a job tomorrow, where to work next, and what your next employer might want to see on your résumé, I suggest you *own your career destiny* by crafting financially rewarding activities that place your interests, needs, talents, and motivators above those of your next employer.

I propose that you continually develop yourself for the work activities that you, not your hypothetical next employer, want to have in your career. When coupled with action to engage in these personally rewarding, income-generating alternatives, this new psychological contract offers a highly attractive degree of freedom. You can work for others while maintaining a commitment and loyalty to yourself and your own professional development. You can leverage the benefits of the new psychological contract by creating your own options—simultaneous, stimulating, and secure career acts.

You can now *get a life, not a job.*

Those Who Have Lives, Not Jobs

People who enjoy what they do for a living tend to *own* their careers in the sense that they themselves have planned, developed, and shifted their career focus to create the stimulating, secure, and balanced work situations they desire. They craft the career acts they like the best, over time. They also have tailored for themselves a sense of financial security by knowing that if one aspect of their career is losing steam (or interest) other career acts can provide a safety net.

In the past, under the old rules of employment, people with multiple career acts might have been criticized for "lacking focus" and "being too easily distracted." Not anymore. In today's employment reality, these individuals are the happiest career professionals I've met because they own their career destiny and do not feel beholden to any one employer. Let's meet a few so you can visualize their working lives:

- Beverly edits books for a mainstream publisher and writes her own mystery novels. In addition to being a writer, Beverly is a tour guide giving tours at a local winery and lighthouse. Not surprisingly, her mysteries and romances are often set at a vineyard or near a lighthouse. In Beverly's case, one career act inspires the other.

- David is a graphic designer and a photographer, with a following among musicians and actors. As a voice-over professional himself, his photography has brought him in the circles of those in the entertainment industry. In David's case, one career act opens the door for another.

- Erin is a successful massage therapist at a gym, a career act she loves. To extend her interest in healing and anatomy, she is also studying to be a chiropractor with a goal to open a private practice. In Erin's case, one career act is helping to fund a future career act.

Like Beverly, David, and Erin, those who are happiest with their careers tend to have multiple sources of income and professional stimulation. They are like you, me, and most people.

Throughout this book, I offer cases of many people who have outstanding careers through their multiple, fulfilling career acts. They run the gamut on almost every dimension, age, education, family situation, and so on. They share a love for what they do for a living. As you will read, their lives are enviable and inspirational—but also highly motivating in their honesty. They provide the evidence that all of us can attain fulfilling lives with multiple career acts. I am inspired by the people profiled in *Get a Life, Not a Job* and hope you will be too.

When you read the profiles of these people, you will notice that some of them work for themselves and some work for others—other organizations, both small and large. The goal of a fulfilling career might be easiest to achieve through entrepreneurial activities because they offer the greatest personal control, but career fulfillment is also possible when you work for an employer full-time. Being an entrepreneur is wonderful for many, but not right for everyone. Thus, although working for yourself can be liberating, *Get a Life, Not a Job* is not a book about starting your own business or finding sources of passive income.

I wrote this book because I have personally enjoyed the benefits of my own stimulating income-creating career acts—and want you to enjoy the same level of professional and financial freedom. I wrote this book because one of my own career acts is "writing books."

A brief sketch of my career acts begins with my occupational field, work psychology: I hold a PhD in industrial and organizational psychology (i.e., work psychology) from Pennsylvania State University. I am a Full Professor of Human Resource Management at Rutgers University in New Jersey (career act #1). After completing my degree and before starting to teach at Rutgers, I developed some international career-related tools that I now use in conjunction with my career counseling practice (career act #2). Over ten years ago, I began a more public side of my career, writing books (career act #3) and giving talks in corporate, military, and nonprofit environments (career act #4).

Do I sound busy? My friends and family members tease me that it seems like I *"never work"* (and I promise that it is not because I am particularly well organized). The truth is I have no idea how many hours per week I "work" because I have crafted my career acts, over time, to include the activities I enjoy, shedding those acts that are not engaging or not designed to move me in the direction of a different, more stimulating career act. More than believing that I print money in my basement, my friends and family members can observe that I have work-life balance, financial and professional freedom, and truly enjoy what I do.

You Too Can Get a Life

Developing great career acts for overall career success is a process, not an outcome. The ability to decide when to shed a career act, when to grow a career act, or when to start a new career act is part of what makes this new approach to managing your career fulfilling, stimulating, and secure.

I do not advocate working longer hours, nor do I want to see you worsen your work-life balance by trying to do multiple time-consuming jobs. What I do advise is for you to devote more energy to building desired or ideal career acts, or one amazing career act, to achieve greater fulfillment. If you have ever worked on a project you found interesting, you know the joy and energy the right career act can give you. Multiple career acts are liberating because they enable you to allocate your time across those career acts you enjoy and shed those career acts you don't enjoy.

Career acts also supply a stress-easing sense of security that comes from knowing if one act of your work-life becomes stale or disappears entirely (as we have seen in many corporate downsizings) that you have other sources of stimulation and income. Your career becomes more nimble and less stressful as your attention can be redirected positively, for personal and financial gain.

The book was written as a step-by-step guide to help you achieve financial and personal freedom. Chapter 1 begins by helping you identify possible income-creating activities that would be liberating and help you make a plan for shedding those you don't enjoy. Chapter 2 helps you discover what motivates you and how you like to work to continually align your career with activities you truly enjoy. Chapter 3 discusses how to build your skills and abilities to advance into more progressively interesting career acts. Chapter 4 specifically focuses on how to make your career acts (or a single career act) as financially and professionally secure as possible from being downsized. Chapter 5 discusses how to bolster your mental, emotional, and physical well-being to manage concurrent career acts. Chapter 6 discusses how you can gain control of your career by effectively leveraging your time, money, and human resources. Finally, Chapter 7 concludes *Get a Life, Not a Job* with some ways to clarify your work-related values and to keep your personal relationships healthy and satisfying while you pursue your career acts.

Get a Life, Not a Job is all about you, a way for you to create a plan to reach your ultimate career goal—enjoying as close to 100% of what you do for a living as possible. I hope you benefit from the insights in this book and have a few "aha!" moments that you can apply to your own career, whether you are currently starting your career, restarting your career, or jump-starting your career.

I look forward to hearing your stories about your career acts; please visit www.PaulaCaligiuri.com to share your career stories with me. With exciting updates every week and new free career tools posted frequently, I invite you to sign up for e-mail updates, to follow me on Twitter (@PaulaCaligiuri), or to become a fan on Facebook (Paula Caligiuri).

Wishing you great happiness in your career success,

Paula Caligiuri, Ph.D.

Create a Personally, Professionally, and Financially Rewarding Career Doing What You Love

"There is no passion to be found playing small—in settling for a life that is less than the one you are capable of living."
Nelson Mandela

Bobby and Tess have multiple career acts. Tess is a nanny during the day and loves to engage in her hobby of photography in the evenings and on weekends. Exciting for Tess, her evening and weekend fun has become increasingly profitable, so she has been gradually cutting back her hours as a nanny. Bobby, her husband, is an IT professional by day. As a second career act, Bobby is a Web designer under retainer to a major corporation, keeping the company's pages current, interactive, and brilliant. He also designs Web pages for others, including one for his wife's photography business. Happy with the way their careers are growing, the couple also reached a personal milestone recently when they bought their first house. Some might think that Tess and Bobby are stretched thin and might experience stress from all they have in motion in their lives. *Would you be surprised to learn that Bobby and Tess are not experiencing stress, even with a new mortgage and a currently shaky economy?* In fact, they credit their multiple career acts with providing them great security in their careers and less stress as they engage in the things they enjoy. Bobby and Tess are busy, and probably could not tell you what was happening in the latest reality TV show, but they are also highly fulfilled doing what they love across their multiple career acts. They are happy as a couple.

The idea of multiple career acts might seem daunting at first. Chances are high, however, that you are already balancing multiple roles in your life. Let's consider the person who has a job and children and provides life care to a family member. This person is already doing the equivalent of three roles. *Are you a student, parent, hobbyist, employee, partner, caregiver, coach, and so on?* This idea of having multiple roles in your life isn't such a huge departure from what most people already do; the idea is just being applied to your career.

The departure, if you will, is allowing yourself to reframe your relationship with work and what you consider the best way to approach career fulfillment. Under the old rules of employment, people with multiple career acts would be chastised by parents, a spouse, or a nosy mother-in-law for "not having a professional focus," "not being serious about your job," "not sticking with it," and "being too distracted." (Ugh!) In today's employment reality, the happiest career professionals allow their talents across multiple career acts to propel their success and security. They confidently ignore these criticisms because they are changing career acts purposefully, and not spinning their wheels hoping for an employer to provide a situation they will find satisfying. They are happy and confident because they are doing what they love and owning their career destiny. *They have lives and not jobs.*

Your career is a large, influential, and time-consuming part of your life. Throughout your adult years, prior to retirement, you will spend almost half your waking hours in work-related activities. If you start working at age 20 and retire at age 65, you will spend 45 years of your life working. You will have, on average, 241 workdays each year and each of those days will include 8.7 hours of actual work[1] for 2,097 hours of work each year. What sane person would want to be unhappy or feel insecure for that much of his or her adult life? Unfortunately, many are.

There are approximately 152 million Americans working in the U.S. labor force today. On any given day, 75% of them would consider changing jobs. In fact, over 60 million of them are actively looking for a new job at this moment. *Are you one of them?* With the downturn in the economy, the elimination of jobs, and the increased desire for work-life balance, people are looking for more stability, greater fulfillment, and increased satisfaction from work. *Are you?*

HAVE MULTIPLE CAREER ACTS AND...

✓ Your career will be managed by you.

✓ Your career will be built on what you love to do—your talents, interests, needs, and motivators.

✓ You will have multiple exciting and professionally stimulating career acts, well integrated into the life you want to live.

✓ You will have more freedom because you will not be locked into any one job or employer.

✓ You will have a greater work-life balance.

✓ You will have greater financial freedom and security.

✓ You will be in control of your future.

Do You Need More Personal and Professional Freedom in Your Life?

Is it time for you to redesign your career—and your life—for greater personal and professional freedom? To answer this question, you need only to think about Sunday night. The way you feel on Sunday nights could be telling you volumes about your relationship with work. *Are you filled with dread for Monday morning? Moody? Anxious? Overwhelmed? Depressed? Are you crankier than you were on Saturday night?* If so, you might be experiencing the Sunday night slump. The source of your Sunday night slump will provide some insight into the relationship you have with work and what might need to change to be more fulfilled in your career. Let's think first about the possible source of the slump:

- *Are you dreading the boredom or monotony of the workweek?*
- *Do you dislike the climate, culture, or people within your work group?*
- *Are you overloaded and overwhelmed with the amount of work that needs to be accomplished?*

If you are experiencing this, what is your level of Sunday night slump? Even those who have engaging and stimulating careers might experience some of these feelings on Sunday evening as they temporarily mourn the loss of their freedom. If your slump is easily mitigated with an episode of *Desperate Housewives*, a football game, or a bowl of Ben & Jerry's shared with a friend, then your reactions are probably not too extreme but are likely telling you that you need to make some changes.

For some of you, the Sunday night slump is more serious. In a poll conducted by Monster Worldwide,[2] over 80% of American and British workers have trouble sleeping on Sunday nights. In addition to insomnia, if Sunday evenings predictably bring more arguments with loved ones, a loss of interest in the things you normally enjoy, and difficulty concentrating, then your Sunday night mood might suggest that something in your life needs to change and you should reframe your relationship with the concept of work.

Please don't ignore these feelings as they are telling you something important about how you are living a big part of your life—and life is too short to be unhappy or unfulfilled in your work life. Allow those Sunday night feelings to help you uncover whether it is time to change your employer, change your job, or transfer to a more satisfying work situation—a multiple-act career.

Why Do So Many People Remain in Unfulfilling Jobs?

"I hate my job." As a career coach, these crushing words will easily launch me into a sympathetic series of rapid-fire questions, with the answers providing the foundation for what I hope will be a creative problem-solving discussion. You're not alone if you feel you are toiling in an unfulfilling job now, with the only hope of someday retiring to start living a more-fulfilling life. The assumption on which the concept of retirement is based—that we need to defer our life's happiness until we reach our senior years—is unfortunate and growing increasingly more illogical under the new psychological contract. *Why do you feel the need to defer your happiness?* Given the change in the psychological contract, without promises for the future return, this delayed-fulfillment approach seems even more absurd. Yet, I have learned, there are reasons why people stay in jobs they hate.

Discussing creative solutions to career fulfillment produces responses on the following continuum: At one extreme, there are the life-is-too-short-to-be-unhappy-at-work folks. They want to approach their careers with fresh eyes. Many (but certainly not all) of them are young adults and those reentering the workforce. The conversation with people at this end of the continuum is always enjoyable, creative, and solution focused. These folks have minimal career-related baggage and want to be happy with whatever they opt to do for a living. They are optimistic and willing to explore possibilities for their careers.

At the other extreme, there are the yes-I-hate-my-job-but-that-is-why-they-call-it-*work* folks. They want to get out of the rut they are in, but have convinced themselves that this is where they need to remain. Many (but not all) of them are experienced and well-trained mid-career or late-career folks. They tend to be bound to an outdated employment scenario that no longer exists. They carry career-related baggage and are pessimistic about exploring options, often not even giving themselves the luxury of daydreaming about other career possibilities.

The latter end of the continuum has taught me much about why people remain in unfulfilling jobs. The five most common reasons are as follows:

- **Financial responsibility**—*"I cannot change jobs now; I make too much money and it would be too difficult to find something at my level. I have too many expenses to ever take the financial risk."* You immediately conjure up the image of an investment banker who is joining the Peace Corps, don't you? The truth is that job changes do not need to be a financial step back, but they might require some planning and preparation so you do not jump before you are ready. When I hear this comment, it tends to be the case that the person is overextended financially and they need their steady current income to pay bills. Any thought of giving that up (even with a new job lined up) becomes an overly daunting financial risk. If you find yourself in this position, try to work on two things concurrently: One, try to get your personal finances under control so you can mentally give yourself license to make career-related choices that are both financially rewarding and fulfilling. Two, develop a budget for the action plan necessary for changing your career.

- **Retention incentives**—*"I only have two more years before I am fully vested in the pension program. I can suffer through anything for a few more years."* The human resources practices designed to encourage retention often work. This is great news for companies hoping to lower their costs to train new workers. This is also great news for those who make it to the goal line with the company and can reap the financial reward in retirement. This is a personal decision regarding whether it is worth it—your call. I'd highly recommend beginning a side career while you, literally, finish "doing your time." If you hate your current job that much, you might feel out of control, and starting a new career act can be both financially rewarding when you make it to the corporate finish line and will be emotionally satisfying, putting you back in control of your career and your future.

- **Fear of change and the unknown**—*"I wouldn't know what to do if I left this job. This is what I know how to do."* Some people truly fear change. Minimally, as humans, we tend not to like it very much. The most successful people I know fear settling *more* than they fear change. They dislike complacency *more* than they dislike ambiguity. We all vary with respect to our comfort level with change and ambiguity. As an individual difference, it really is not fair for me to offer pithy suggestions in the hopes of turning the most cautious into a career bungee jumper. If you really hate your job (slightly more than you hate change), I would suggest not changing a thing in your current work situation—but, rather, add a small additional career act, rooted in something you love. You can then control when and how (and if ever) your job will change by dedicating more time to this additional career act. When you feel comfortable and the change no longer produces anxiety, you'll make the leap.

- **Escalation of commitment (or misplaced loyalty)—** *"I have worked in this profession for 15 years; I am not about to give up the years I have put in to start over."* *"I have given a lot of myself to this organization."* These are such retro comments. Sorry for the repetition, but it does warrant repeating. The psychological contract between employers and employees has clearly changed. Employers have no long-term commitment to their employees and employees should feel no sense of long-term commitment to their employers. Your employer owns jobs; you do not. There are no guarantees that "your" job will be there in the future, just as there is no expectation that you will stay with the organization if there is a better opportunity for you elsewhere. There are no gold stars for attendance in this stage of your life. Please move on if you are truly unhappy. There are bound to be better opportunities elsewhere, especially ones you create for yourself.

- **Pessimism—***"It is naïve to think you can like what you do."* *"I do not believe there are any fulfilling jobs—work is work."* I feel sorry for those who really believe this is true. If you are not a natural pessimist, the underlying sentiment is usually related to a lack of creativity for your options. This book should help with that and, if you fall into this pessimistic category, I'd suggest you start talking to people who genuinely seem to enjoy what they do for a living. They are out there—but don't take my naïve word for it.

Being fulfilled in your income-generating career activities is critical for your emotional and physical well-being. Life is far too short to spend time in a job you hate, and your happiness does not need to be deferred to your senior years. It is time for you to get a life, not a job.

Simultaneous Career Acts, Stimulating Options

As a work psychologist and a career counselor, I am well aware that having a satisfying career takes some serious, planned, and purposeful work on your part. Especially during these difficult economic times, giving advice on building and managing careers is rather sobering.

Life is complex, but thinking of your various income-generating activities as career acts *can lead to an exciting, balanced, and fulfilling career, and one with a safety net or two.* I have many rapidly shifting career acts myself, but this isn't about me; *this approach is all about you and finding what fits best in your life for your talents.*

Let's start by having you think of those people in your life whose careers you know well and admire most. *Do their careers possess any of the following features?*

✓ **Do they have multiple professional career acts?**—The individuals who have the most fulfilling careers often have jobs across a variety of career acts. Some of these individuals have multiple *related* career acts: the mechanic who rebuilds classic cars for clients, the sous chef who gives cooking classes in her home, the orthopedic surgeon who invents a new prosthetic device, or the aerobics instructor who is a personal trainer. Other individuals have multiple *unrelated* career acts: the nurse who runs a weekend cake-decorating business, the teacher who runs an online antique tools business, or the engineer who owns and manages several rental properties. They each have multiple career acts. Each career act is independent and potentially interesting.

✓ **Do they have options in their lives?**—The individuals who are the most free from the bonds of an unhappy job have options in their careers. If you have the ability to leave your company at any time, you earn the right to operate with more freedom and flexibility within the career act. Individuals with multiple career acts tend to not be bound to any one company for their paychecks. They might enjoy their jobs and want to stay with their companies—but they do not need to do so. The difference is exceptionally liberating.

✓ **Are they unique and central to the success of their organization?**—The individuals who have the most fulfilling careers are central to their organizations, across their career acts. These individuals tend to have unique skills and personal characteristics that are difficult to replace—and others recognize this. They are critical to the success of the career act or the business— and, again, others recognize this to be true. Those with successful careers are not necessarily the most senior individuals in the organization—or those with the greatest number of degrees—but they do know how they contribute to the organization's success, and they have a realistic sense of their value across each of their professional roles.

✓ **Do they talk about their careers in ways that sound stimulating, interesting, and energy giving?**—People who love what they do draw energy from the career acts they are in. Instead of dreading the idea of going to work or working, they actually look forward to it and enjoy it. I promise this is a reality for some people (you might even know a few). I want it to be a reality for you.

Professional and financial freedom has never been as critical as it is today in 2010. As I write this, the unemployment rate in the United States is about 10%. Even during a period of lower unemployment, however, having a multiple-career-act life will enable you to obtain greater fulfillment from work given that the sources of this fulfillment are spread throughout your multiple career acts.

I do not advocate working longer hours or toiling in multiple jobs. Multiple dull career acts would still result in a dull (and more stressful) life. I also do not advocate running yourself ragged trying to do multiple jobs (even if they are engaging). I advocate finding multiple income-creating activities that you sincerely enjoy, that fit with your life in a fulfilling, balanced way, and that offer you financial freedom because you are not relying on any one employment setting.

20

Finding Your Career Acts

Think of your current primary job (or the one you seek) as career act #1. *Do you have any other income-creating activities in which you engage?* These can be activities such as running an eBay business, working a weekend landscaping job, giving guitar lessons, or selling your paintings at the local art festival. If you have any income-producing activities, outside your primary career act, those are your additional career acts. Use Exercise 1 to think about your own current set of career acts.

Exercise 1: Your Current Career Acts

Career act 1 is likely your full-time job or the job that offers your greatest source of income.

Your other career acts are any additional sources of income, such as a part-time job, contract work, an extension of your first career act done in a different venue, a profitable hobby, passive income (for example, from a rental property), and the like.

What are your current career acts?

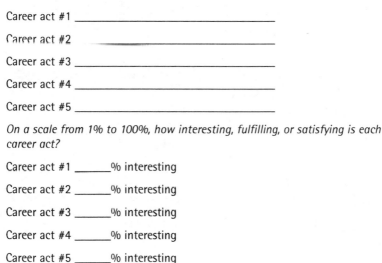

Career act #1 _____

Career act #2 _____

Career act #3 _____

Career act #4 _____

Career act #5 _____

On a scale from 1% to 100%, how interesting, fulfilling, or satisfying is each career act?

Career act #1 _____% interesting

Career act #2 _____% interesting

Career act #3 _____% interesting

Career act #4 _____% interesting

Career act #5 _____% interesting

21

Adding all lines to 100%, what percent of your total annual income is derived from each career act?

Career act #1 _____% of my total income

Career act #2 _____% of my total income

Career act #3 _____% of my total income

Career act #4 _____% of my total income

Career act #5 _____% of my total income

If you are like most people, only the line for career act #1 is filled, and it is only 10% to 50% satisfying—but it accounts for all of your total income. If you have additional career acts, these are likely your most interesting career acts (between 75% to 99%) accounting for less than 10% of your total income. If you filled in career acts #2 and #3, chances are you indicated that your career act #1 provides income while the additional career acts provide only satisfaction. Although that is a reasonable place to start, you probably agree that it is far from the ideal career situation.

Over time, as you develop your career acts, you will begin to see these indicators shift. Your goal will be to derive more satisfaction from the career act in the center of your life while earning an increasing percentage of your total income from the additional career acts. As you do this, your career will become more stimulating, balanced, and secure. Use Exercise 2 to plot your own income-to-satisfaction ratios for each of your career acts.

Exercise 2: Plot Your Satisfaction-to-Income Ratio over Time

Career Act 1	Now	In 6 Months	After 1 Year	Etc.
On a scale from 1 to 100, how interesting is this career act?				
What percentage of your income is derived from this career act?				

Career Act 2	Now	In 6 Months	After 1 Year	Etc.
On a scale from 1 to 100, how interesting is this career act?				
What percentage of your income is derived from this career act?				

Career Act 3	Now	In 6 Months	After 1 Year	Etc.
On a scale from 1 to 100, how interesting is this career act?				
What percentage of your income is derived from this career act?				

How to Create a Career with Multiple Career Acts

To begin to develop your multiple career acts, you first need a primary career act—a place to start. This starting point will vary tremendously depending on many factors: the extent to which you are in a current job you enjoy, whether you have the skills you need to start your ideal career, whether there are hurdles for starting your ideal career (e.g., license, degree, training), and so on. In a nutshell, you need to start somewhere while paying your bills—so you might as well begin purposefully.

To start, let's acknowledge that you need to pay the bills. Any would-be actor who has waited tables in anticipation of a big break will attest that you might not be able to experience your most fulfilling

23

career act immediately. Instead, you need a career act that puts food on the table and keeps the lights on; if it also provides benefits such as insurance and paid vacation, even better. It might be a temporary or seasonal job, a project-based assignment, or an entry-level position, but it is a place to start. This will, over time, generate income and help you start additional career acts by offering a financial base or a platform from which you can develop your skills.

A note of caution is also in order: Although adding a boring part-time job might increase your financial bottom line (and might be a necessary short-term move at some point in your career), this will not lead to greater enjoyment, fulfillment, or balance. A person with an interest in physical fitness might be well suited to begin a career act working at the desk in a health club. Staying in this desk job at the health club without concurrently pursuing a fitness training certificate or a degree in nutrition, however, is not recommended. The best-managed careers acts become progressively more liberating and offer an increased sense of work-life balance. To use a sports metaphor, keep your eye on the ball and continually grow your career acts purposefully.

Your plan for growing your career might vary depending on which of your career acts you are considering. You might be very advanced on one aspect of your career but at the most entry-level stage in another. If you are starting from the beginning on one of your career acts, and have the luxury of spending time pursuing interests, don't shy away from unpaid opportunities because you never know where they can lead. An interest in live theater might motivate someone to take a starter job working in the ticket office at a regional theater. Taking an unpaid internship at a sports magazine or volunteering at an animal shelter are great starter career acts for those with a passion for sports or animals. The venue and being around others who share your passion are great starter career acts—as long as you know how you can grow from there.

Remember that the concept of a multiple-act career is a process for managing your career, not an end state.

Adding Career Acts Ethically

Many people add career acts based on something they have been doing professionally, an extension of their current role, perhaps with another organization. This is common and logical because a current employment situation might have helped you increase your level of expertise and skills. Before discussing how to grow your ideal career generally, let's discuss the ethics of the noncompetition among your career acts—especially if your primary career act is working for an organization. Consider the following five rules for adding career acts ethically:

1. **Avoid conflicts of interest**—Career acts should be, ideally, separate industries so you are not tempted to (or unintentionally) compete with your current employer, independent contracting, or freelancing activities. If your career acts are in the same industry, try the "newspaper test": *If your career acts were on the front page of the newspaper, would you be embarrassed?*

2. **Do not borrow time, knowledge, or materials**—If it feels as though you are overstepping your bounds "borrowing" from one employer or client site in an effort to build a different career act, you probably are. This might be as seemingly innocuous as checking e-mail for one career act while billing or being paid by another—or it might be as blatant as taking supplies from one career act for use in another. Try the "manager or client test": *Would you be comfortable telling your manager or client about your activity without any concern?*

3. **Be sure you are not violating your contract**—If you work for one employer or if you signed a contract as an independent contractor or freelancer, your career acts might

be limited (usually with noncompete clauses). Even if you did not sign a contract when you began working, you should check in your organization's policy manual or, more difficult to learn, the expected implicit norms of the organization.

4. **Report income honestly**—If you work for an employer in the United States, you will receive a W-2 form, including your income and some deductions, such as federal and state taxes and Social Security. If you work as an independent contractor, you should receive a 1099 form from each of your clients throughout the year. If you do not receive a 1099 from a given client or organization you should keep a record of income earned and expenses to accurately report your income for tax purposes (for example, if you receive less than $600 from an organization they do not need to generate a 1099 for you but you will still need to report the income). As an aside, if you do much work outside of traditional employment settings, I would also suggest you speak with a tax professional to be sure you are receiving all of the possible tax deductions.

5. **Do not poach clients**—If you freelance and are employed in the same area where clients would be identical, you might experience a conflict of interest, which could be perceived as poaching clients. As before, try the "manager or client test": *Would you be comfortable telling your manager about your conversations or work with clients without any concern that he or she would view them as a conflict of interest?*

Approaches for Adding Career Acts

Now that you know the ground rules for building career acts ethically while working in another organization, you can start to consider different ways to build a more fulfilling career through multiple career acts. The following sections discuss four.

Approach 1: Leverage Your Expertise or Talents

What do you do or know that would be valued by others? What is your area of expertise, something you know more about than others? What skills and abilities do you have that you can leverage? With a little creativity, your answer to any of these questions could provide the foundation for a possible career act. To make the transition, you will want to gain a sense of the possible market demand for what you hope to offer, whatever your income-generating career act might be. Let's look at a couple of examples.

Jay's career acts—Jay has worked for over 25 years with the same employer in various consumer electronics engineering roles, an occupation he greatly enjoys. Over the past 8 years, he has worked specifically as the director of quality engineering within the division of a company that does digital image processing. As the director of this unit, he has gained unique expertise in being able to identify the type of device (make, model of a camera, mobile phone, etc.) that has taken a specific photo by being able to interpret encrypted data in the image files. Because of his unique knowledge, Jay was asked to provide some expert testimony on digital photo images that were to be used as evidence in a court case. When Jay accepted the invitation, he found that he enjoyed the courtroom experience and took satisfaction in knowing that he was contributing to the justice system. Jay has now leveraged his expertise into another career act as an expert witness, a person who can provide expert testimony on the source of digital images.

Dan's career acts—Dan works full-time as the director of development for a philanthropic organization. In earlier stages of his career, he has worked for a variety of nonprofit organizations where he has been successful in writing and winning large grants. As a volunteer firefighter in his town, he has also written and won grants for his fire company. With a clear track record of success, Dan has been able to leverage his grant-writing skill into a profitable and fulfilling side business, providing grant-writing services for multiple noncompeting nonprofit organizations that are unable to afford a full-time grant writer.

Jay and Dan both leveraged their expertise and talent, extending their reach to create additional career acts. If you really cannot identify your expertise or talents, ask your friends. Often, others see our talents more clearly than we see them in ourselves.

Approach 2: Expand a Hobby, Interest, or Passion

What do you enjoy as a hobby? Do you have any passions or interests that could be expanded into a side business, a career act? Having a profitable hobby, interest, or passion can be one of the most enjoyable ways to make a living, especially if you can turn it into a thriving small business. *Who wouldn't want to generate substantial income doing what they love?* The world is full of people who have done just that— they've taken their hobbies, originally enjoyed solely for personal pleasure, and turned them into income-generating career acts. Hobbies with tangible outcomes, such as art, sewing, baking, cooking, photography, playing a musical instrument, and the like, can easily move to income-generating career acts. Let's consider the following fabulous examples:

Monica's career acts—Monica was unfulfilled in her career as a corporate organizational development specialist for about 6 years when she was (unfortunately?) laid off. She instinctively knew that she did not want to go back to a full-time corporate job, only to be unfulfilled in her career again. After a trip to Nepal where she hiked Mount Everest and contemplated life, she decided to follow her passion into something gardening-related. Monica had been doing garden coaching for friends for about 7 years—mostly for free or in exchange for a good bottle of wine and a dinner—and had taken a lot of courses toward that career act. In fact, she is currently finishing a certificate program at the New York Botanical Garden in Environmental Gardening. She loves teaching others about gardening and started a garden coaching practice, created a Web site on local gardening resources (including newsletter and blog), and is currently developing an online store selling semicustom garden plans to novice gardeners and new homeowners. Monica started by building a Web site on local gardening resources (www.thegardenerslist.com) then going around to all the local nurseries to tell them about it. She started a gardening newsletter distributed to local nurseries as well as through e-mail to a growing list of subscribers. She plans to offer advertising in it next year. (Advertising will be a great source of passive income.) She uncovered an interest in Web site development and search engine optimization and started a consulting practice on these interests. Monica also does about 3 days each week of management consulting, allowing her great flexibility to run her own businesses.

Tom C.'s career acts—Tom works full-time for a large organization in the information technology (IT) field. As a client development manager, he is considered highly valuable by his organization because he is in a wealth-creating role for his firm. Tom has worked in similar roles for a variety of IT companies over his 30-year career and in the process has earned much professional freedom over time. While employment in the IT industry is still a fulfilling full-time career act, about 15 years ago Tom began buying rental properties and currently has 7 homes, fully rented. He is mechanically inclined and handy, enjoying the occasional maintenance and odd jobs the rental properties require.

Tom also has an interest in green energy technology and has, over the past 10 years, developed a line of electric bicycles. Knowledge of electric motors and building electric bicycles was a self-taught hobby, one he enjoyed tinkering with all of his adult life. Inventing and marketing electric bicycles is Tom's primary passion and, currently is a third career act, which he hopes will become more central over time.

Terry's career acts—By occupation, Terry is a nurse. She has been a nurse for almost 30 years and (on many days) still enjoys what she does. She recalls sharing that she wanted to be a nurse for as long as she can remember and cannot imagine doing anything else. As a hobby, Terry also loves to design and sew—she says her prize possession is her much-loved sewing machine. Terry's passion for sewing is personal. She has rarely accepted money for the beautiful things she creates for her family and friends. But in the past few years, the circle of Terry's "friends" has expanded beyond its real limits. As much as she enjoys sewing, she decided that she needed to start charging for her time and creative effort. Although reluctantly charging at first, Terry found that acquaintances were more than happy to pay for her creations, and now her second career act thrives.

Clearly Monica, Tom, and Terry have multiple career acts and multiple sources of income. Do you, as Monica, Tom, and Terry, have a hobby, passion, interest, or talent you would like to turn into an income-generating career act? Try Exercise 3.

Exercise 3: Career Acts Based on Interests, Hobbies, Passions, and Talents

Name your hobbies: _____

- How could I be paid while doing this hobby?
- Realistically, what steps would it take to do this ideal job?
- What are the paths to reach the goal of that ideal job?

Name your interests: _____

- How could I be paid while enjoying this interest?
- Realistically, what steps would it take to do this ideal job?
- What are the paths to reach the goal of that ideal job?

Name your passions: _____

- How could I be paid while pursuing this passion?
- Realistically, what steps would it take to do this ideal job?
- What are the paths to reach the goal of that ideal job?

Name your talents: _____

- What are you good at—what do others say you are good at?
- How could I be paid and leverage my talents?
- Realistically, what would it take to do this ideal job?
- What are the paths to reach the goal of that ideal job?

Monica, Tom, and Terry have stories that make profitable hobbies sound easy. For most people, profitable hobbies really are an enjoyable way to make money. But, before you dive in, consider the following three (often overlooked) issues:

1. **Understand the psychological shift**—You are now working for clients, not engaging in a hobby for yourself. You might lose freedoms enjoyed as a hobbyist when you begin to have customers or clients. I have a friend who bakes wonderfully and periodically talks about baking full-time. When pressed on why she doesn't, she says that baking is her "release," her way to unwind at the end of the day and she does not want to lose her "release" by placing client demands on her baked goods. This is insightful and highly relevant for those who view their hobby as a personal outlet and would not want to fill orders to customer specifications. Alternatively, you can take a different approach and create what you like, hoping you'll find clients or customers who will appreciate and purchase what you want to sell. In this case, the trade-off is the preservation of personal freedom enjoyed as a hobbyist for a potential limitation on your range of clients or customers. Your call—just think it through.

2. **Know how to value your time along with the tangible costs to price your goods or services**—Even if you only want to engage in your profitable hobby for a few hours each week, value your time as if you were doing this full-time. Try this: Ask yourself: *What income would I (realistically) want to be making if this was my sole source of income?* Divide this out to an hourly wage and multiply by the hours you spend on one unit of your profitable hobby. Add in overhead. Add in material costs. Add in taxes. Decide what profit you would like to make (taking into account your level of skill, experience, etc.). Too many

people undervalue their time and their other intangible assets (such as their skill level).

3. **Know your competition**—Hobbyists can operate in a delightful bubble; they can be blissfully unaware of the cost, quality, or marketability of whatever they produce. *If I want to make melted-bottle spoon rests for myself, family, and friends, do I really care about competition? No.* When you begin to market your hobby as a source for potential income generation, be sure you understand the competition and the potential market, the demand for your goods and services.

Monica's, Tom's, and Terry's hobbies are tangible and seemed to easily move to income-generating career acts. *What about less-tangible hobbies, interests, or passions, such as a general interest in travel, food, sports, or Groucho Marx memorabilia?* One of my favorite examples of a less-than-tangible interest turned into a career act is Jennifer, a Web designer who happens to love coffee. One of her favorite coffeehouses was a privately owned café where the proprietor roasted his own coffee beans. After becoming acquainted with the proprietor as a regular customer, Jennifer set up a Web-based business to market the very coffee she enjoys.

Honestly, I have a hard time with the question *"What are your talents, passions, interests, and hobbies?"* My most sincere answer is that I don't have any hobbies. My passion, if you will, is spending time with family and friends in interesting or beautiful places. Whether I am with my family at our lake house in upstate New York or with friends in Tuscany, I am most engaged when I am with wonderful people in great places, doing interesting things. This doesn't translate easily into a career act—at least I haven't yet found someone who will pay me for this. Thankfully, there are other approaches to adding career acts.

Approach 3: Pursue an Occupation

Occupations are a series of related jobs within job families that share a set of knowledge, skills, and abilities. Doctors, plumbers, actors, and teachers are examples of occupational groups. Within a given occupation, skills are generally transferable across a variety of work situations. For example, a physical therapist might have a private practice and might also work part-time for a minor-league baseball team or might work one day a week at a rehabilitation center. A teacher might offer English as a Second Language classes to new immigrants or tutor. If you are interested in exploring possible occupations, consider engaging in the following activities:

- Visit industry Web sites to learn more about selected occupations.

- To explore occupations that might be a good fit for you, you could also take some assessment tools to determine your interests. One very popular test is the Strong Interest Inventory. You can visit www.careers-by-design.com/strong_interest_inventory.asp to take the Strong Interest Inventory. Another one is ACT's Discover program found at www.act.org/discover.

- Speak to individuals who are currently in occupations or jobs you believe you would want. People, for the most part, enjoy talking about what they do for a living, especially if they are passionate about their jobs.

- Join professional online forums designed for people interested in certain professions, industries, and so on.

- Another great source of information about occupations is O°Net, where you can look up almost any occupation and find out a world of information, including tasks performed; required areas of knowledge, skills, and abilities to perform the job; and the context of the work. O°Net's Web site is http://online.onetcenter.org/.

Approach 4: Generate Sources of Passive Income

At the risk of sounding lazy, this is my personal favorite. A very wealthy and successful friend once said to me when I was thinking about a career in consulting, *"Paula, people never get wealthy exchanging time for money."* His advice was, and remains, excellent. Our time is a 24-7 limited resource. The amount of time you want to use each day on income-generating activities is one more value to consider when crafting your ideal career acts. Think about the life you want to live and answer the question seriously: *How much time do you want to spend engaging in career acts?* If you are like many, you might be laughing at the question and answering "as little as possible." If so, I'd recommend you consider ways to develop a career act or acts to provide sources of passive income (money that is paid to you for a product or service that does not require your active involvement or time).

Monica's newsletter where she is able to sell advertising and Tom's rental properties are examples of passive income. We discuss ways to create passive income in the last chapter of this book.

Great career acts are as diverse as the people who occupy them. These four approaches produce wildly different careers in people with multiple career acts. They are often combined and reconfigured throughout our careers to achieve ever-increasing career satisfaction. More than anything, you want your career to have a trajectory of positive growth in satisfaction and fulfillment. Please give yourself time to explore the many possibilities available to you. Once identified, you can use Exercise 4 to help you make the plan for growing your career acts.

ART CENTER COLLEGE OF DESIGN LIBRARY

Exercise 4: Planning and Growing Your Career Acts

Your Ideal Career Act #1

- Possible starting career act:
- Knowledge, skills, and abilities I need for this starting career act:
- Different ways I will gain them:
- The next step after this starting career act to move me closer to my ideal career act:
- Possible derailers and ways to proactively address them:
- My timeline:

Your Ideal Career Act #2

- Possible starting career act:
- Knowledge, skills, and abilities I need for this starting career act:
- Different ways I will gain them:
- The next step after this starting career act to move me closer to my ideal career act:
- Possible derailers and ways to proactively address them:
- My timeline:

Your Ideal Career Act #3

- Possible starting career act:
- Knowledge, skills, and abilities I need for this starting career act:
- Different ways I will gain them:
- The next step after this starting career act to move me closer to my ideal career act:
- Possible derailers and ways to proactively address them:
- My timeline:

The Necessary Elements for Multiple Fulfilling Career Acts

Your fulfilling career acts will be personally, professionally, and financially rewarding and based on what you love to do. Although no two people have identical career acts, great careers share five fundamental elements:

- **Self-awareness**—Your interest in occupying various professional roles and the centrality they are given will change over time. Know yourself well and identify your talents, interests, hobbies, passions, needs, motivators, and how you like to work. Give yourself permission to expand or change your career acts if you are not fulfilled or as your life changes. The goal, if you will, is the growth and movement toward ever-increasing career happiness.

- **Continuous self-development**—No one is born with the knowledge, skills, and abilities for every possible interesting career act. Be honest in assessing your knowledge, skills, and abilities and be open to actively learn and develop. You might need to practice an act (in an unpaid internship or volunteer situation) to gain the necessary skills. You might need to accept a starter career act to gain skills. Remember, this is a dynamic process to move you closer to a career that is well integrated into the life you want to live.

- **Unique and critical roles (especially critical for those in single-act careers)**—It might be the case that your ideal career has only one act: one great career act where you will derive 100% of your career satisfaction—either as an entrepreneur or while working for an organization. This is the riskiest approach to managing your career for all the reasons mentioned earlier, but certainly not impossible. If you want a one-act career, please be amazing, make it a career you love, and have a safety net. This safety net is your uniqueness to

37

your business and your centrality to your employer, your customers, or your clients.

- **Well-managed time, money, and human resources—** Multiple-act careers grow strategically, with one career act funding the development of another, more interesting act. One career act might free up time for another. Make a career plan, revisit it frequently, and revise it when needed. Your career plan will have some logical steps with financial and professional goals as milestones. If you like to cook, you can think about developing your career acts in the same way you would prepare and cook a dinner. Each dish needs some different ingredients and needs attention at various times.

- **Harmony among your work, family, and personal life**—Multiple-act careers leverage interests, needs, and motivators. When done well, your career acts are purposeful and you are in control. As the person in control of your life, you are in charge of where your time and energy will go. Your career is only one piece of your overall life, and no one other than you (especially not an employer) should be crafting how you want to live your life.

The next five chapters delve deeper into each of these elements, offering some practical advice on how best to create and manage your multiple career acts.

chapter two

Discover What Really Motivates You

"The biggest adventure you can ever take is to live the life of your dreams."
Oprah Winfrey

A student starts his first professional job. A midcareer professional is downsized from her company. A stay-at-home parent returns to the workforce when his child starts school. An employee is frustrated in a dead-end job and wants to quit. Each case involves a person at a different life stage with different personal and professional circumstances. Each case involves a person making a career change.

The stage of your career and the reason for wanting a more fulfilling career is less important than the mind-set and the willingness to plan your career acts. Your career acts will involve taking some well-planned professional risks to grow into increasingly more satisfying roles. Staying in control of these moves in your professional life will involve another element—knowing yourself, your needs, and your motivations well enough to understand how you like to work and what engages you in your work.

Starting, Restarting, or Jump-Starting Your Career

The quote *"insanity is doing the same thing, over and over again, but expecting different results"* has been attributed to Benjamin Franklin, Albert Einstein, and Rita Mae Brown. Regardless of which luminary wrote it, the quote clearly describes today's most current career advice, especially for new graduates and those at the start of their careers. They are advised to start their careers with organizations that will "look good" on their résumés. These ideal starter jobs, as the advice generally goes, should be with "banner" organizations with widely known high-selection standards. In business, these banner organizations are large and stable firms, such as GE, Goldman Sachs, IBM, Pepsico, and other blue-chip companies.

Tenure and steady promotions at banner companies, according to this standard—but outmoded—career advice, signal success to any future employer: Banner companies on your résumé will signal that you have been selected into (and survived) the high standards of well-respected firms. *Have you been given this advice?*

GET A LIFE, NOT A JOB ADVICE

✓ Don't settle for a mediocre career if you are motivated for a more fulfilling one. Keep moving.

✓ Timing is critical. Strategically shift from one secure position to another more interesting and fulfilling one.

✓ Stay in control by changing before you are forced to change (e.g., through downsizing or a layoff).

✓ Don't waste time hoping for a change in a current unfulfilling work situation. Bad situations rarely change into great ones.

✓ Don't be afraid to change. Great careers involve some risk.

Although well-meaning, this advice is based on an old psychological contract intended for a world that no longer exists. This advice is aimed at seeking the approval of future employers rather than maximizing your own professional satisfaction and personal fulfillment. This advice sets new graduates up for career frustration, almost guaranteeing that they will soon join the ranks of the 75% of Americans who are unhappy with their careers.

The advice that you should value the name of your employers over the pursuit of your own career fulfillment is insanity if the intended goal is overall life satisfaction. In my opinion, this advice is especially ridiculous for newly minted graduates who are full of energy and enthusiasm (and generally light on financial or familial commitments). They, more than any others, should begin by filling their first career act with something they find exciting while concurrently thinking about how they might expand their other acts.

The perpetuated myth rooted in the old psychological contract lulls students (and all of us) into falsely believing they should have a linear path between their education and their career fulfillment. One piece of advice I give enthusiastic new graduates is to not fear the process of creating their own career story. I offer this because many twentysomethings in this generation value personal freedom and work-life balance— but expect these to be fulfilled through traditional employment relationships (i.e., the myth of the old psychological contract). Young adults will never be able to have the freedom and balance they value using their parents' (and grandparents') outdated relationship with work.

Many young adults (and many people, in general) are not comfortable owning their career destiny because they either believe it will take too much time (infringing on their highly valued personal freedom and work-life balance) or they lack the efficacy and do not believe that this is possible (no one ever gave them the license to have

41

this type of bold relationship with the idea of work). The latter is much easier to address because I believe we all can have the careers and lives we want, as long as we are willing to make some fundamental changes in the way we approach our relationship with work. The former concern (it takes too much time) baffles me because we will spend the same amount of time (more or less) working in jobs we dislike when compared with working in jobs we enjoy. Crafting a career, however, is an active process—not a passive one—requiring more engagement but not necessarily more time. Let's consider Joshua's career acts; his story is a great illustration of purposeful changes and also a healthy self-awareness of how he likes to work and what motivates his career moves:

Joshua's career acts—In college, Joshua began his passion-based career acts by combining his interests in both music and journalism. To pursue a career in music journalism, he volunteered to intern (for free) at *Rolling Stone Magazine*, while simultaneously building a Web site for a contemporary music composer. Within a few months, Joshua used the skills gained in his unpaid internship to begin building Web sites for pay, and his first career act began. Meanwhile, after he gained experience and saw the realities of what he had thought would be an ideal career act at *Rolling Stone Magazine*, Joshua decided that this was not going to be fulfilling and was not the career act he wanted. While continuing to build Web sites during the day, he returned to school to pursue another interest, a master's degree in music and interactive technology. His thesis focused on the social and cultural aspects of technology creation. Upon graduation, Joshua changed career acts and began a successful and growing career with an online cross-cultural training company (which he enjoys very much) because he values the collegiality, creativity, and challenge in his work. His passion for music provides an additional career act, as he plays in a band on weekends.

Individuals restarting their careers, such as those who have spent a few years as stay-at-home parents or those who have been unemployed for a while are in a similar situation to new graduates because they are able to start afresh crafting their careers—this time (hopefully) with a multiple-career act approach. If you are in a dual-career household, having another household income is the most liberating way to start a multiple-act career because you have both financial flexibility and some lead time to plan for this transition. Let's consider an example:

> **Linda's career acts**—Linda became a grammar-school teacher after graduating from college. When she and her husband had their first child 8 years later (they eventually had three children over the next 6 years), they decided that Linda would be a stay-at-home parent until their children were finished with school. When the time came for Linda to reenter the workforce, she opted for multiple career acts. She began by using her teaching credential to tutor special-needs children in her local school district. Her interest in learning disabilities and her love of teaching made this a good fit for her first career act. She has been able to expand to a related second career act by beginning a private practice, instructing her associates on her preferred methods of tutoring. Although Linda's first two acts are closely linked, her third act is very different: She conducts cultural debriefs for families moving to international locations. She originally began this work when a friend who consults with companies sending employees on global assignments was overloaded with debriefing work. The friend noticed Linda's verbal skills and insightful nature. These attributes, along with her interest in working with individuals one-on-one and her love of international experiences, combine to give Linda a rewarding third career act.

In contrast to new graduates and those with an employed spouse, the luxury of timing and planning is generally not afforded to those who lose their jobs unexpectedly, whether they are fired, laid off, or downsized—and have no financial safety net. Perhaps the best evidence of the broken psychological contract is in the faces of those employees truly surprised that they have been fired or had their position eliminated. In hindsight, they might wish they had jumped from the employer before they were pushed, but now they are in midair and need to land gracefully. If you are in this situation, after you have inhaled with panic, try to exhale with relief that you are now able to start fresh with a more satisfying career.

Finding yourself unexpectedly unemployed can wreak havoc on your self-esteem and emotional well-being. As Americans, we often tie our self-worth into what we do for a living. The following are some tips for protecting your psychological health while starting a more fulfilling career after a layoff:

- **Be realistic about the job search process**—The rule of thumb for finding a new job is that it generally could take about 1 month for every $10,000 you are hoping to make in salary. In this current job market, it could be longer. *Do you have any hobbies or outside activities that could transition into income-generating career acts, even temporarily? Can you find a temporary part-time job that will serve as a starter role toward an ideal career act?*

- **Schedule your day**—Treat your jobs search just like a regular full-time job. Wake up early, have breakfast, shower, get dressed, and so forth. Whatever your normal routine would have been when you were working, keep that daily routine. The only difference is that the eight-hour workday should be spent on activities to build your career acts.

- **Schedule your evenings**—Don't listen to friends or family members who say that because you are home all day, you must be well rested and relaxed. This can be a stressful time, irrespective of location. Spending eight hours each day building career acts can be stressful. Manage your evenings with low-cost or no-cost activities to help you relieve that stress. Eat a healthy dinner.

- **Develop all of your career acts**—Falling into the same one-job/one-employer rut seems like a safe pursuit. However, if possible, do not default to this immediately. Remember, the psychological contract has changed and it is up to you to create excitement, balance, and fulfillment in your career. Consider starting or developing activities across several fields of interest, rather than just one. Rather than feeling like a victim, try to reframe the layoff into an opportunity—a chance to explore your multiple possible career acts concurrently.

- **Consider ways to perform career acts in more meaningful ways**—While reworking your career acts, consider adding some acts of charity or volunteer opportunities that will be consistent with your overall long-term career goals. Volunteer to sing in your church choir if you find satisfaction in singing. Walk dogs at the animal shelter if you love animals. Even if one or two of your career acts are volunteer roles, you never know where the activities might lead.

- **Apply for unemployment benefits and manage your financial reality**—Depending on the realities of your financial situation and the amount you will receive from unemployment benefits, you might still need to take the first available job to make ends meet. Think about how this temporary or part-time job might fit in with one of your long-term multiple career goals. For example, if you plan to take a job as a store clerk temporarily, and one of your passions is sports, why not try to get a job in a sporting goods store?

I hope you will never be asked to leave the security of a current employer before you are fully ready. My recommendation is to prepare mentally today for the possibility that this might happen in the future. You own your career destiny, so look out for yourself by developing other acts of your career in alignment with the things you love to do, your talents, your needs, and your motivators. Given that you have options and alternative acts, a multiple-act career will give you greater financial freedom and flexibility. It will help you to own your career and stay in control, regardless of what happens. Let's consider how Karen did this:

Karen's career acts—Karen worked for a large pharmaceutical company in marketing. She was dedicated and proud to work for her banner company and was rewarded with steady promotions and outstanding performance reviews. But recently she found herself unexpectedly downsized when the company sold her division. In a tight labor market, she had few prospects for another marketing job at her level. With mounting bills at home and unemployment benefits about to run out, she decided to take a job at a much lower pay level. Certainly this was not ideal, but Karen decided that if she would work for less, at least she would work in an environment she enjoyed, interacting with people. She took a temporary part-time job at a high-end department store selling women's designer fashions, where she enjoyed the environment, the clients, and the clothes. Soon Karen realized that many of her customers had closets full of good-quality clothes that they were no longer willing to wear, and began to think about the possibility of opening a consignment shop. Her hope was to offer designer clothes to women who could not afford to buy them brand new, but appreciated the quality and style. For about six months, she built inventory of clothes by calling friends who she knew had very nice designer wardrobes. Most were thrilled to clean out their closets and possibly make some extra money when Karen's shop opened. Her spare bedroom looked like a retail warehouse. She bought a professional-grade steamer and several heavy-duty rolling racks for clothes. When Karen was certain she had enough of an inventory to open the store, she rented a well-located (but very small) space in a nearby strip mall. She and her husband designed and decorated the space themselves. She strategically advertised her grand opening, inviting friends to increase the perception of volume. Her talent for marketing, her high standards, her easy nature around people, and her sincere love for designer clothes made her consignment shop steadily increase in sales. Within one year, her shop became her primary career act and she is now thinking of opening a second location in another town. Looking back, Karen is actually thankful she was downsized from her pharmaceutical marketing job.

Like Joshua, Linda, and Karen, give yourself permission to pursue something you love and work in a way you most enjoy. Remember, you are not working for the lines on your résumé. You are working for you. You are in control of your career.

I encourage you to turn back to Chapter 1, "Create a Personally, Professionally, and Financially Rewarding Career Doing What You Love," and, if you haven't already done so, work through the exercises, thinking of multiple career acts as you start, restart, jump start, or change your career entirely. Having multiple career acts based on the things you want to do will eventually lead to greater freedom and professional satisfaction. Remember, a multiple-act career is a dynamic process, not an end state. It evolves over time and, like Joshua's feelings when he left *Rolling Stone Magazine*, none of these career acts are set in stone. The roles you occupy can—and should—change whenever your career act is causing you an unacceptable level of prolonged boredom, frustration, anxiety, or stress. Great career acts will give you energy! (I promise.)

Finding the Best Context for Your Career Acts

As we discussed in Chapter 1 and in this chapter, the premise of a multiple-act career is to align your career, in multiple ways, with your interests and occupational preferences. This section dives deeper into how you like to work; the needs, drives, and motivators you have; and how those affect the way you should craft your career acts.

Do you know how you like to work? Some people have a general idea of how they would like to work (that is, the context) rather than what exactly they would like to do. If you really do not know how you like to work, you can use the fitting-room method: Try on many before selecting the right one. Robert did just that:

Robert's career acts—Robert's family wanted him to be a doctor. During high school and college, he worked in a hospital to learn whether he really wanted this occupation (quickly realizing that the sight of blood made him queasy). Robert's father was a builder and real estate developer. During summers and vacation time, he worked with the carpenters and learned the business from the ground up but wasn't sure this was the right occupation for him. What Robert did know was that he wanted to be a leader and develop an organization in the industry he chose. While in college, in addition to working in the hospital and as a carpenter, Robert worked in a restaurant as a waiter and bartender and in a department store as a salesperson. He did not mind working his way up and learning as he went, but he wisely was interested in understanding the vibe of the industry. After his 6-year occupational tour while in high school and college, he realized that he did not find an industry he enjoyed more than real estate development. Almost 25 years later, he is partners with his mentor and idol (his father) in a successful real estate development business. Robert loves what he does.

Robert knew he wanted to lead and build an organization. He knew the context, but not the industry. This is true for many people. Have you ever met someone who says, "I could never work a desk job," or "I like this small company," or "I like knowing that I am helping people." If so, you are hearing contextual preferences without hearing what they do. Again, this is typical for many people, so let's explore them.

The next sections explore two contextual issues you should consider as you craft your career acts—your needs and motivators and how you like to work. Chances are high that your ideal career acts will be some combination of what you want to do with how you want to work.

Career Acts Based on Your Needs or Motivations

Career acts differ with respect to individuals' personal motivators or needs regarding their work. Some individuals are motivated, for example, by achieving challenging or "stretch" goals, whereas others are primarily interested in building close relationships at work. It is important to understand what motivates you because the match between your needs from your career and the work you choose will affect how satisfied and fulfilled you feel doing what you have chosen to do.

Dr. David McClelland[1] has an interesting theory of human needs that can be applied to our careers. Dr. McClelland believes that we each have varying degrees of three primary needs: achievement, affiliation, and power. These needs are shaped through our earlier lives and are relatively stable across situations. They would have implications for the type of work we would enjoy.

- **Need for achievement**—If you have a high need for achievement, you do not give up easily and will work very hard to achieve your goals. You thrive in competitive situations and will enjoy outperforming your coworkers if it means that you can distinguish yourself (and be promoted). You like to work toward your goals and prefer to succeed on jobs that require the use of your abilities and skills, rather than chance or luck. You do not hesitate to assume additional responsibilities, particularly when they allow you to demonstrate your achievements.

- **Need for affiliation**—If you have a need for affiliation, you actively participate in social activities and enjoy being liked and considered as an important member in a group. You enjoy working with friends and are motivated by working with others. You tend to accept people readily and make an effort to build friendships and maintain contacts with coworkers. You tend to initiate, participate in, and facilitate social events in the workplace. Team-building activities, corporate retreats, and work-related social events are highly motivational for you.

- **Need for power**—If you have a need for power, you are highly motivated by opportunities to lead others and have influence. You tend to have a strong desire to take control, influence decisions, and direct the work of other people. You might seek out opportunities for leadership roles and assume them very naturally. Motivators that indicate power or authority (for example, job titles and leadership development programs) will generally be highly motivating for you.

As these needs suggest, your ideal career acts might have nothing to do with talents or passions, but might be rooted in the fulfillment of your deeply held needs. At my local North Brunswick, New Jersey, post office (I am not kidding, the post office), there is a team of postal clerks who are collectively the happiest work group I have ever observed. At the risk of being accused of not getting out much, this is what I have observed: They genuinely like people and seem sincerely happy to interact with customers (regardless of how cranky the customers are when they walk in); they genuinely like each other (this is difficult to fake and easy to observe while waiting in a long line); and they are engaged in their work and want to help. (Frankly, I don't need any more help with using the automated postal system— but they seem so eager to help that I accept the assistance.) You do not need an advanced degree in psychology to see that the members of this team of postal clerks each have a high need for affiliation. Between their interactions with customers and with each other, this need is met for each of the clerks.

In addition to need fulfillment, another way to think about your career preferences is through the model developed by Dr. Edgar Schein.[2] Dr. Schein proposed that we each have our own set of career anchors, those values or drivers that motivate us to seek and ultimately find satisfaction with our work situations. You can consider the following sidebar to begin thinking about your career needs and motivators. For an assessment and interpretation of your career anchors, visit www.careeranchorsonline.com.[3]

Career Acts Based on the Way You Like to Work

You might be reading these past two sections and thinking: "None of this applies to me; I just don't have dominant passions, interests, talents, needs, or motivators." I can accept that, at least in part. *Do you have a better time articulating what you don't like, compared with what you do, when it comes to work-related activities?* If so, you may have significant work preferences, and you are not alone. Many people can be very happy in their career acts by simply having the opportunity to work as they like to work—not driven by any desired occupational category, interest, or industry. *Are there some tasks you enjoy more than others?* If so, these likes are your work preferences. Let's consider some questions that might shed light on your ideal career acts from the perspective of the way you like to work:

DR. EDGAR SCHEIN'S CAREER ANCHORS

- **To be a technical or functional expert?**—Would you like to be so good at what you do professionally that your expert advice will be sought continually?

- **To be a leader or manager of people?**—Would you like to be in charge of a business unit, making decisions that affect many people and managing the efforts of others?

- **To be autonomous or independent?**—Would you like to have the freedom to do a job your own way and on your own schedule?

- **To be secure or stable in your job?**—Would you like stable employment and financial security?

- **To be entrepreneurial or creative/innovative?**—Would you like to start and run your own business?

- **To be dedicated to a cause or to feel that you are serving a greater good?**—Would you like to make a real contribution to humanity and society, using your talents in the service of others?

- **To be competitively challenged?**—Would you like a career in which you can solve problems or compete in situations where few can excel or win?

- **To have work-life balance?**—Would you like a career that will permit you to harmonize all important aspects of your life (e.g., your personal life, your family, and your career)?

- **To have an international career?**[4]—Would you like a career that enables you to work in different locations around the world and with people from diverse cultures?

- **Knowledge recall**—Do you have a great memory and like to gain and recall information? Or, do you prefer tasks that do not require the recall of knowledge?

- **Knowledge acquisition and problem solving**—Do you like to solve problems, creating new knowledge and understanding what was not previously known? Or, do you prefer tasks with known solutions or procedures?

- **Task duration**—Do you like short-term tasks, those that change rapidly? Or, do you like long-term projects, ones you can focus on—or get lost in—for hours or days?

- **Predictability and structure**—Do you like the repetition and the comfort of knowing what is coming next, along with the satisfaction of seeing things completed? Or, do you like when tasks change rapidly, forcing you to be in the moment?

- **Group work**—Do you like working in a group, where many share knowledge and input for an outcome or join collectively in the creative process? Or, do you like working alone, getting lost in your own thoughts and creative energies?

- **Service orientation**—Do you like helping others, providing service, or making people feel better? Or, do you like working in ways that do not involve client interaction?

- **Physical movement**—Do you like being in motion, either using your physical strength or moving from place to place?

Chances are good that you were able to answer many of these questions. Now, think about your current job or any past job and reanalyze what you did—and did not like—about those jobs. Select a few occupations that seem interesting and ask yourself whether these align with your answers of how you like to work.

Self-knowledge of the way we like to work is critical for finding our ideal career acts. Let's think about these occupations: A doctor, personal trainer, claims adjuster, and dishwasher repairperson have stored knowledge, recalled and applied when needed. They differ dramatically in the physicality of their work and the duration of their tasks. They differ in their levels of stored knowledge and necessary recall. In another example, a journalist, actor, police officer, and housepainter all have knowledge about the techniques of their professions, but their job situations change frequently. They differ, however, on the level of customer service and teamwork necessary in their roles.

Having Multiple Career Acts Based on What Fulfills You, Your Motivations, and How You Like to Work

As the previous sections noted, there are many ways to decide your career acts, including your interests, occupational preferences, career needs, motivators, and a basic knowledge of the way you like to work. As with all great careers, you need to make decisions while being honest with yourself and gathering data about yourself, what you enjoy, what makes you happy, what really interests you, and what motivates you. Let's consider the following examples:

Chikako's career acts—Chikako was hired by a large investment bank immediately after completing her undergraduate degree in psychology. Although she was a highly successful performer within the bank, after four years she realized she did not feel fulfilled at all in her job and needed a change. She had originally selected psychology as her major because she wanted to help people or serve the greater good, a career motivator that was not being fulfilled at the bank. Likewise, her creative and artistic interests were also unfulfilled. With a greater awareness of her own desire to work for a greater good and her passion for art, she returned to school to become an art therapist. This became Chikako's first career act. Her second and third career acts are both currently developing, and they stem from her hobbies and interests. Chikako loves yoga and travels internationally to practice yoga with world-renowned yoga masters. She has started training to be a yoga instructor, an investment in her second career act. Recently, she began substituting for yoga instructors who were on vacation and was an instant favorite among her yoga students. Her second career act began. As a ceramic pottery artist, Chikako is being encouraged (perhaps cajoled) by her friends to begin selling the beautiful pieces she makes, which are currently collecting dust. If, eventually, she decides to sell her remarkable ceramic art, this will become her income-generating third career act.

Marc's career acts—Marc works for a local auto parts store. He enjoys his job, in part because he enjoys helping customers find what they need and in part because he enjoys his colleagues. The store has a relaxed and cordial climate and he is a very social person. Marc is considered the "go-to guy" when a customer comes in with an unusual request. A few years ago, Marc started an online business where he sells auto parts for antique and classic cars. He enjoys the thrill of the chase (no auto pun intended) trying to fill his online customers' requests. He surprised himself at how much he enjoys the search process, trying to locate exactly what people need. He sincerely enjoys both the search and knowing he is helping others.

Tom M.'s career acts—Tom has an advanced degree in mechanical engineering and is currently a professor at a research university. Before pursuing his job in academia, Tom worked for 13 years in various research and development jobs. His career has been focused, almost laserlike, on his belief in his inventions, medical devices for heart patients. Tom incubated his inventions in his partially finished basement with his young children acting as lab assistants and his wife, also an engineer, working on the team. He believed in his inventions before anyone else did and was passionate about eventually seeing his primary invention, an intricate drill to shape a catheter, someday help save those who have had strokes or heart attacks. When Tom applied for and was granted an academic position, it was to return to his love for research. Tom worked with his university's innovation center, enabling him to set up his laboratory in real lab space and start his business. He now has a small business, a spacious new laboratory, and research assistants. His natural extroversion and his passion for his work make his classes in thermodynamics, heat transfer, fluid mechanics, and biofluids some of the best in the department. The products from his new laboratory are fulfilling his need to see his inventions help people who are suffering from heart disease.

Chikako configured her first career act well, combining her interest in art and her motivation to help others. Her second (and possibly third) career acts grew from strong interests and hobbies, yoga and ceramic art. Marc and Tom both had single-focused interests that developed into career acts. Marc's love for cars and knowledge of where to source rare auto parts gave him an additional source of income with his online business. Marc is social and enjoys helping customers—but also enjoys the process of tracking down items. Tom's inventions have allowed his career path to take him down the road to be both an academic and an entrepreneur. Both of these career acts allow for considerable autonomy and personal freedom, the way Tom enjoys working.

As Chikako, Marc, and Tom did, I encourage you to configure your career acts based not only on your talents, interests, hobbies, passions, and occupational preferences, but also on your needs and motivators and how you like to work. This will take some personal reflection and self-awareness. To help facilitate this self-awareness, I encourage you to reflect on the lists in this chapter and work through Exercise 5. There are also Web-based tools on www.PaulaCaligiuri. com that can help you with this process.

Career Acts Based in Your Reality

On September 18, 2007, Professor Randy Pausch of Carnegie Mellon University gave a lecture, a lecture that would eventually be heard by millions but written for his three young children. Randy's lecture motivated us to dream again and inspired us to stay true to those dreams. The lecture and the book, titled *The Last Lecture*,[5] touched millions of hearts around the world because he spoke of how he had lived his childhood dreams, encouraging us all to keep our own childhood dreams alive and make them come true. He spoke with urgency to a world desperate to dream again. He spoke with authority as someone who had successfully lived his childhood dreams. He spoke with credibility about life because, at 47, he was, in fact, near death. Ten

---

Exercise 5: Career Acts Based on Your Work-Related Needs, Motivators, and the Way You Like to Work

In deciding the type of career you would ideally like, consider your career needs, motivators, and how you like to work. Does any pattern emerge?

Your Career Needs and Motivators:
• Career Need and/or Motivator 1: _____
_____
_____
• Career Need and/or Motivator 2: _____
_____
_____
• Career Need and/or Motivator 3: _____
_____
_____

How Do You Like to Work?
• Preference 1: _____
_____
_____
• Preference 2: _____
_____
_____
• Preference 3: _____
_____
_____

months after delivering this lecture, Randy died from pancreatic cancer. Randy's illness gave the world a gift, the license to dream and not apologize for wanting to fulfill those dreams.

I believe many of us lose our ability to dream about fantasy careers somewhere in our late teens or early twenties, the time when the dominant message is that we should "get serious about our future." This advice throws water on the fire of our young adult passions as we concede that we're unlikely to become a supermodel, professional football player, ballerina, or rock star. This career concession is also rooted in awareness of our personal realities: We discover that there are people who are more beautiful, more athletic, better dancers, and better guitarists. We start to see our realities—and, perhaps (for the first time), the limits of our own skills and abilities.

But there is a wide open space between an "unattainable dream career" and a "get serious career" that should still allow plenty of room for creativity to fulfill the underlying motivators of why we held a certain dream. We just need to root our career dreams in the realities of our natural skills and abilities—and the probability that we can attain the career act.

Ask yourself two questions:

1. **What would your ideal career be if you could do whatever you wanted—anything at all—without being limited by your own skills, abilities, or probability of success?**—If you are having a difficult time answering this, try having the conversation with some close friends. (Think of this as a purposeful cocktail conversation.) Those we love can often be more creative with our talents and abilities than we can for ourselves.

2. **Why is this career so appealing?**—Be honest. There is no one here to judge you. (You might want to leave the friends out of this part of the exercise.)

For example, if your answer to question number 1 was to become a "race car driver" or "television star," your answers to the second question will provide the clues to more attainable and potentially also highly fulfilling career acts (just in case #1 does not work out, of course). Let me provide some examples of what I mean by alternative careers that would be equally fulfilling.

You want to be a *race car driver* because...

- *You love speed*; an alternative career might be *airline pilot.*
- *You love the adrenaline rush of driving fast*; an alternative career might be *firefighter.*
- *You want to meet the beautiful women who present the trophies at the end of the race*; an alternative career might be *fashion designer.*

You want to be a *television star* because...

- *You want to be wealthy*; an alternative career might be *investment banker.*
- *You want to be on television*; an alternative career might be *broadcast journalist.*
- *You want to meet actors*; an alternative career might be *talent agent.*

Exercise 6: Career Dreaming in Reality

Name your dream, ideal, or fantasy career_____ .

1. This is a dream career because _____

1. An alternative career to this end could be _____

2. An alternative career to this end could be _____

3. An alternative career to this end could be _____

2. This is a dream career because _____

1. An alternative career to this end could be _____

2. An alternative career to this end could be _____

3. An alternative career to this end could be _____

3. This is a dream career because _____

1. An alternative career to this end could be _____

2. An alternative career to this end could be _____

3. An alternative career to this end could be _____

Start with a dream, ideal, or fantasy career act. Understand the underlying motivations for this career desire. Think of plausible alternatives that would also follow from the same motivators. *Are you noticing any patterns across your dream careers?*

You see how this works. Now, try it out for yourself with Exercise 6. If you visit www.PaulaCaligiuri.com, there is also an online and interactive version of this exercise you can use to understand your talents and the motivators underlying your career dreams.

How Can You Tell Whether an Ideal or Dream Career Act Is Realistic or Out of Reach?

In career counseling, you will rarely hear me utter the words to suggest that a person's career dreams are unrealistic. At the risk of sounding like Pollyanna for a moment, I do believe most can achieve what they would like from their careers. That said, I live in this world and know the process is beyond some people's reach. From these same career-counseling sessions where I won't tell people not to have dreams, I can almost always predict those who will make their dreams a reality. You can apply the same diagnostic to yourself:

1. **What is your ideal career in terms of the need for underlying natural abilities and do you possess them?**—Careers vary on their requirements of our natural abilities. Some careers are bound by natural ability, whereas others require very little natural ability and can be achieved as a function of raw motivation. "Becoming a professional athlete" is an example of the former. "Becoming a millionaire" is an example of the latter. In some cases, there really is a natural limit for the given career act. I am short and in my 40s and, by nature of the occupational requirements, will not ever be a supermodel or a professional athlete. Very few professions are bound by their requirements on our natural abilities.

2. **Do you have the strength of character to overcome doubters and naysayers?**—The self-fulfilling prophecy comes into play in force when you are told that your dreams

61

are unrealistic (especially when the words are uttered by those who are trusted). It is not surprising that many people lose their ability to dream about careers as young adults, when they are starting their careers or unemployed. At a younger age and during a career crisis (such as a period of unemployment), people are particularly vulnerable because they often have less efficacy for their careers, unfortunately, listening to the well-meaning advice of others who don't want to see them disappointed. This collectively results in lower efficacy and in a self-fulfilling prophecy for unrealized career dreams. This is a big one. If you don't think you can achieve your dream career goal, I promise you never will.

3. **Are you realistic about the dream career and what it will take to achieve the career?**—Some of the most glamorous careers involve periods of tremendous boredom or tasks that are less than glamorous. *Do you really know what it means to have your dream career? If the answer is yes, do you have a plan for achieving it?* Those who are unrealistic about the career or the process are concerning. Outside of Hollywood movies, dream careers do not happen overnight. Have well-articulated, reasonable, and measurable goals to guide the path to your dream career. If you know what you are getting yourself into—and know what it takes to get there—any dream career can become a realistic career goal.

In this chapter, you've seen how you can change or add career acts to follow your interests, passions, talents, and motivations. This chapter gave you some questions to ask yourself so you pursue career acts most consistent with your needs and motivations and the way you like to work. This chapter also gave you some license to reconnect with your childhood dreams and carry them over to your adult ambitions. (Remember there is likely some secret to your adult happiness embedded in those childhood dreams.)

Reflect on the first two chapters and give yourself some time to find the right career acts, with the realization that an ideal career act might not be rooted in talents or passions or dreams; they might be rooted in the fulfillment of needs and motivations. In trying to discover your ideal career acts, allow yourself plenty of freedom to explore possibilities. These first two are tough chapters for many people. Take your time with the process of self-discovery because identifying career acts is not a small first step. You are welcome to visit www. PaulaCaligiuri.com to use the interactive career tools available to help you indentify your ideal career acts. Once identified, the next step, offered in Chapter 3, "Propel Your Career Forward through Self-Development," is to explore how to aim for success in each career act.

chapter three

Propel Your Career Forward through Self-Development

"I don't think much of a man who is not wiser today than he was yesterday."
Abraham Lincoln

If you have ever marveled at the strength and agility of Cirque du Soleil performers, you can fully appreciate the time and training that must be involved in their acts. Your acts will not require you to twist yourself into a pretzel (literally or figuratively), but great career acts generally require some investment of time, mental energy, and possibly money (for education, training, equipment, and so forth). Career acts do not become great overnight: You need to develop knowledge, skills, and abilities to make them great.

As you review your ideal career acts, think about what might be needed to steadily improve each career act. *Do you know what knowledge, skills, and abilities you will need for each career act? Can you identify them readily?* The three most common ways to identify the knowledge, skills, and abilities needed for various career acts is to read, observe, and talk.

Reading about Your Ideal Career Act

Many outstanding books and Web sites are available to provide information on the knowledge, skills, and abilities needed for any given career. Even a simple Internet search will produce a wealth of information. The Vault has a useful Web site (www.Vault.com) and an excellent series of books about various careers, occupations, and professions. Their material is particularly helpful because it outlines not only the knowledge, skills, and abilities, but also the ways that careers typically progress. From the Web, you can also access job posting boards on various Web sites to better understand the type of knowledge, skills, abilities, education, and experiences that employers seek.

If you are interested in investigating possible careers from the comfort of your home or are interested in trying to figure out how to strategically break into a given industry, I'd highly recommend exploring the competency models created by the U.S. Department of Labor and the Employment and Training Administration in collaboration with various industries leading professional associations. The site www.careeronestop.org/CompetencyModel offers the competencies needed for a career in a variety of industries. These competency models offer hints on the knowledge, skills, and abilities you should possess to land a starter career act in your selected industry—even at the entry level.

Observing People in Your Ideal Career Act

I highly recommend you observe those individuals who are currently engaged in your ideal career. Shadow someone on a typical workday. I suggest you *not* choose a close friend or a family member because they, although well-intentioned, might offer the type of evaluative information you should be concluding on your own. Try to shadow multiple people and the same people on multiple days—because the same career acts might change depending on who is in the role and the day you are observing.

Talking with Someone Currently in Your Ideal Career Act

It is fortunate for us that people love to talk about themselves and, therefore, it is relatively easy to gain information about careers. Again, avoiding family members and friends if possible, try to set up interviews with those who are currently in your ideal career act. Most people enjoy talking about what they do and how they achieved their career success—and often feel flattered that you consider them successful and want to emulate them. Try to interview multiple people in the same career act. Have a structured set of questions about their career path; the knowledge, skills, and abilities needed for the career act; and their thoughts on how the career might be changing in the future. See Exercise 7 for guidance on interviewing people in your ideal career act.

Exercise 7: Asking the Right Questions of Those with Your Ideal Career Acts

Here are some questions you can ask those with your ideal career act:

1. How did you attain your current career? Is your path typical or atypical for those in your career?

2. What experiences or education prepared you for this role? What experiences or education do you wish you had that would have made your career even more successful?

3. Do you know others in your same role? If so, how did they become successful in this career?

4. What are some things most people do not realize about this career?

5. If I wanted to do exactly what you are doing, what steps would I need to take? What are the factors impeding success at each step? What are the factors facilitating success at each step?

The Knowledge, Skills, and Abilities for Your Ideal Career Acts—Where You Are Now and Where You Need to Be in the Future

We believe it was Socrates who gave us the sage advice approximately 2,500 years ago to "know thyself": This is especially useful if you are interested in developing your career acts from a realistic assessment of your knowledge, skills, and abilities. *Once you know what an ideal career act might need, how do you know the relative level of your current knowledge, skills, and abilities compared with what is needed?*

After a dozen years and countless opportunities to work with individuals who are striving for more fulfilling careers, I have learned that moving from self-awareness to career success is challenging for almost everyone. Self-awareness is a critical, but not small, first step. The following are some observations that impede individuals in their ability to move from self-awareness to career act success:

- **Internalize self-awareness data accurately**—Listen to karaoke or an overly confident person after a job interview and you can quickly hear that some people have a bloated perception of their strengths. At the opposite extreme, some people refuse to believe they possess the raw talent that others see in them. Given that most successful people often possess a modicum of humility, the arrogance end of this continuum is what is chiefly concerning. In either direction, I encourage you to strive for *internalized accuracy about your personal strengths and developmental needs.*

- **Not everyone can fully develop useful strengths**—Try as I might to be a professional basketball player, I will never overcome my 5'3½" stature and the fact that I have virtually no natural athletic ability. (Being selected last in gym classes since the first grade was fairly consistent 360°

feedback for me.) Volumes have been written about the relative mutability of knowledge, skills, abilities, and other personal characteristics. At a minimum, we know that some are simpler to change than others; for example, gaining knowledge about the rules of basketball is easier than improving eye-hand coordination. For some career acts, personality characteristics such as openness, extroversion, and emotional stability underlie many necessary competencies for success. Personality, however, is typically more difficult to change. It is important to *consider the level of mutability that underlies the various strengths you aim to develop.*

- **Opportunities to develop strengths are not always readily available**—Developmental opportunities to build necessary strengths can happen in traditional venues such as apprenticeship programs, training centers, and universities or through a variety of self-initiated situations. They might take time, such as engaging in an unpaid internship to gain entry into a desired occupation, organization, or industry. They might take money—colleges, universities, and training centers can be expensive. They might take other resources not readily available in your current situation. Part of developing the skills needed for your career acts is to plan for these challenges. Some of *the best opportunities to develop skills might be bound by time, money, or opportunity.*

The following sections discuss some other ways you can gain an accurate awareness of your knowledge, skills, and abilities.

Feedback from Others

The Internet now provides a vehicle for us to receive feedback for many things we do, especially those things we do that touch the lives of others, from how well we sell an item on eBay to the helpfulness of the recipe review we posted. Unfortunately, however, this feedback is generally not of the kind most of us can readily use for improving our career acts (unless, from my previous examples, we are opening an eBay business or becoming a professional recipe, music, or literary critic).

Gaining self-awareness about our knowledge, skills, and abilities through feedback from others requires an effective vehicle for open, honest, constructive, and multisource reviews—ideally from those people who are in the best position to judge our performance. Teaching evaluations are structured feedback tools to assess professors' class performance. Organizational performance appraisals, especially 360° feedback tools (where performance is rated by supervisors, subordinates, peers, and possibly clients), provide a structured method to identify strengths and areas for development. Customers and clients vote with their wallets, but often do not provide feedback on ways to improve our knowledge, skills, and abilities unless we follow up with client satisfaction surveys or ask for feedback, specifically addressing our role in the sale or providing service.

You can also increase self-awareness about your knowledge, skills, and abilities through more informal feedback. *On what activities do you receive the most compliments or the most negative comments, either in or out of work?* Encourage opportunities to debrief with your colleagues. Pay attention to their messages and then self-reflect on the knowledge, skills, and abilities that either facilitated or impeded your performance. Try to seek as much honest and constructive feedback as possible from multiple people who are in the best position to evaluate your knowledge, skills, and abilities.

Interactive Tests to Evaluate Your Knowledge, Skills, and Abilities

The Internet is full of "tests" to assess yourself on everything from your readiness for marriage to your ability to effectively detect serial killers by looking at their headshots. Although these might be entertaining, or even useful for a certain type of detective work, neither is likely to prove particularly useful assessing your knowledge, skills, and abilities for future career acts.

The problem is that although there are many tests available, not all are good. In fact, today it is so easy to make a test look professional that it is becoming increasingly difficult to tell which ones are legitimate assessment tools. Before wasting your time taking (or, worse, paying for) a test or assessment tool online, consider the following:

- What entity is marketing or promoting the test or assessment tool? If it is a reputable organization, association, or institution, it is probably (but not always) an effective tool. Reputable organizations will promote tools with scientific evidence, especially if they list research published in peer-reviewed scientific journals.

- Are any of the psychometric properties of the test given, such as reliability or validity? Both reliability and validity are critical test attributes on which assessment tools or tests should be judged. These tell us whether a test is an accurate measure of a given skill or ability (reliability) and whether the test scores relate to an external measure of performance (validity).

- Was the result of the test consistent with the feedback you have received from others about your knowledge, skills, and abilities—or about what you know to be true about your knowledge, skills, and abilities?

As an alternative to online testing, consider seeking out a qualified career counselor who is trained and experienced in giving aptitude tests. The benefit of working directly with a counselor is that you get not just your test scores, but also a proper interpretation of what they mean and how they apply to your particular career situation and goals. Many colleges and their alumni associations and some professional organizations have career counseling departments and will provide this service for a reasonable fee. You can also access professional career counselors who work independently. As a word of caution, please ask for references and contact those references to learn more about any given counselor's effectiveness. The field is currently not a regulated one, which means that anyone is able to call him- or herself a career planner, career coach, or career advisor without any need for certification or qualifications.

Evidence and Patterns of Success

Without the benefit of feedback from others or the objective results of an assessment tool, you are still able to acquire an accurate assessment of your knowledge, skills, and abilities. Ask yourself the following questions:

- What are the activities in which you have most often succeeded (or failed) throughout your life?
- What are the activities that are consistently successful (or unsuccessful) whenever you engage in them?
- In which activities do you seem to track better (or worse) than those around you?

Now that you have the information about your various knowledge, skills, and abilities relative to those needed for success in your future career act, do you see any gaps you need to close? The next section talks about how to close the gaps relative to what is needed for your ideal career acts.

Improving Your Knowledge, Skills, and Abilities for Your Future Career Acts

If you believe there is a gap between your current set of knowledge, skills, and abilities and those you need for your ideal future career act, the next step is to work to close that gap. You can gain knowledge and build your skills and abilities in a number of ways. Here are a few:

- Gain knowledge through reading books, credible Web sites, and articles. Try to apply your knowledge as you believe you are gaining it to gather some realistic feedback on whether you are, in fact, closing the knowledge, skill, and/or ability gap.

- Apprentice or intern with someone who has the knowledge you need to gain or can help you develop your skills and abilities—*and is willing to teach you*. If you are fortunate, perhaps the apprenticeship or internship can be a paid opportunity. If you will be in this activity as an unpaid opportunity, try to squeeze every developmental drop from the experience. This is an investment in your future career acts.

- Take a job as a starter act to build your skills for the future. If you are interested in a particular industry, for example, you might need to accept a position that will give you greater knowledge about that industry or practice applying your skills to the new industry.

- Take training classes to enhance or build a knowledge base, skill, or ability. Embedded in training programs are opportunities for feedback from an instructor or, at a minimum, an opportunity for you to compare your own knowledge, skills, and abilities against those of the others in the training class.

- Seek a professional coach who can work with you on improving the gap you hope to close. Some coaches can also facilitate your entry into a given career, such as a career coach or agent. This person should be effective at providing honest feedback and able to offer suggestions for what you can do to improve.

- Go to college for a degree or advanced degree. Although expensive, great university programs well known for the occupation you seek are sought out by employers as feeder pools for well-qualified job candidates. These great programs build their reputation on being able to place their graduates into their desired careers. The success of this strategy is based on three things:

1. You are reasonably certain this is the career act you want. University education can be expensive, so you don't want to waste money on an education that leads you down the wrong path.

2. You select a university that is well known for your desired ideal career act, especially for advanced degrees.

3. You do well in the program. (Yes, recruiters do speak with faculty members and ask for their opinions.)

A Cautionary Note about Investing in a Degree

Attending college for a degree or an advanced degree is a very typical way to create a starter career act. Universities can often help their graduates get their feet in doors of employment situations the students could not possibly enter on their own. In college, you will gain knowledge, learn skills, and hone abilities to help in your career act. Colleges and universities are wonderful institutions, rich in opportunities and sources for professional exploration. Colleges and universities cannot, however, create your ideal career for you. Too many students enter colleges and universities with this incorrect expectation. Education is not a passive process.

As a university professor, you might find it odd that I am continually mystified by students (and their parents) who pay exorbitant college tuition bills with only limited knowledge of what exactly they are buying. It is crazier than buying an expensive house from a picture posted on the Web. (At least with the house, there is a picture of what you are buying.)

Try this: Ask a college student (or ask yourself if you are a college student), *what are your tuition dollars buying?* The answer tends to fall into one of three categories.

Group 1: The *I Want to Be a...* Group

For this first group, they know that their degree is a first step in a chosen career act. As educated consumers, the especially savvy ones in this group will have researched placement rates (and can probably recite how their university stacks up to others). Universities with highly ranked degree programs in the student's chosen field are always the best bet for those in this group as these universities will have the best relationships with prospective employers and top graduate schools or professional schools. If aggressive enough, these students can network with the best in their chosen field (alums and professors) from day 1 of their college experience. With tenacity and a willingness to work hard, the path to their starter career act is paved.

Group 2: The *I Want to Learn* Group

The students in this group really don't know what they want to have included in their career acts and are not bashful about using their college years to learn about and explore their options. As educated consumers, the savvy ones in this group are willing to attend every possible career night, meet with faculty members, network with alums, audit classes (just because they sound interesting), join clubs, take unpaid internships, network some more, and pursue just about everything to squeeze the most out of the experience. They might change their major many times but, ultimately, they will get their money's worth and walk away from their college experience knowing what they enjoy, how they like to work, what comes naturally, and the career path to pursue that will be most fulfilling. They will have an idea or two (or ten) for possible starter career acts and they will have many contacts to help them open doors. In my opinion, large, in-state research universities with oodles to offer are the best for students in this category because they offer many options, and the students can explore (perhaps an extra year or two) without going too deep in student loan debt.

Group 3: The *I Dunno* Group

This is the group I worry about. I worry about their debt. I worry about their parents' debt. The students in this category tend to stumble into a major and graduate with a degree they can't quite figure out how to use in a field that does not excite them very much. They might enjoy their college experience but don't use it to explore their career options. After graduation, they take a job out of necessity when student loans start to become due and wonder, shortly after graduation, whether their degree was worth it. The exploration opportunities available in their college years slipped away unused.

Yes, college education has many financial and professional advantages over the course of one's career. This has been established in many studies. However, those graduates most able to leverage the many advantages of a college education are in the first two groups.

Times have changed: College is very expensive and the current job market cannot easily accommodate those who are not leveraging college to create their own professional opportunities. My fear for those in Group 3 is real, especially if they are attending private or out-of-state universities with their associated high tuition bills. Although financial aid is widely available, the average student loan debt is about $21,000.[1] This amount is not exorbitant if doors are opened on starter career acts. However, a college degree does not guarantee a starter career act.

A 2009 poll by CollegeGrad.Com asked college seniors: *"Do you think you will have an offer in hand by graduation?"* 84% said *"no."*[2] The National Association of Colleges and Employers reports that employers plan to hire 22% fewer college graduates from the class of 2009 than they did from the class of 2008.[3] These stats are sobering. Kudos to the students in Groups 1 and 2: They tend to fare better in this tough economy because they have used college to create opportunities for great career acts.

If you think you might be in Group 3, the *I Dunno* group, I encourage you to adopt the behaviors of Group 2—or wait a few years to go to college and use those precollege years to explore some options so you can return to school with the certainty for a starter career act as those in Group 1.

Building from Starter Career Acts

Whether a college experience, a part-time job, an internship, education, or anything else that could be considered a starter career act, try to reframe your approach and consider it an opportunity to grow and learn. When well selected, these are the acts that lead to more fulfilling career acts. Often they are described as "doing your time" or "paying your dues," both having negative connotations. These phrases also have the image of passivity, as if you have no choice but to "do time" or "pay dues." Multiple-act careers are all about choice and personal decision making. If you accept a low-level or low-paid position to learn about an industry, gain some exposure for an occupation, or develop the knowledge, skills, and abilities needed for the future, then these are active starter career acts—not at all passive. You need to engage while you are in these starter acts to reap the benefits from them. Let's consider some examples:

Janet's career acts—From an early age, Janet was interested in beauty, modeling, and fashion. She loved the industry but knew she could not be an elite, high-fashion model because she wasn't tall enough. To move closer to her area of interest (and before she knew what she wanted to do with her

GET A LIFE, NOT A JOB ADVICE

✓ Be realistic about your current and necessary skill level to succeed in your ideal career acts.

✓ Invest in yourself by developing your skills—the greater the valuable skills you possess, the more control you will have over your career.

✓ You should continuously improve your skills and abilities. Especially in science and technology, skills that were considered leading this year might be passé in a few years.

✓ Don't be afraid to try new career acts that look interesting. Remember this is a dynamic process and your interests might change over time.

✓ The best career acts require you to take some risks or make some investments in yourself.

career), she took a job as a part-time receptionist at a small local modeling agency in her city. Although she did not realize this at the time, this was her starter career act. Janet answered phones and made copies and did many of the tasks that, in a different context, would have been mind-numbing. But Janet was intentional about using this experience to squeeze every ounce of knowledge out of the owner of the modeling agency. The owner, seeing Janet's dedication and engagement, was willing to give her increasing responsibility, even inviting her to participate in some makeup and runway classes. She enjoyed the classes but realized she was finding greater fulfillment from the business side of the agency, booking models. Over time, Janet was promoted and began her primary career act as a modeling agent. After she married, she moved to a different city and started her own modeling and talent agency. Janet is highly successful today doing what she loves, and readily admits that she learned everything she knows about the model management business from what began as her part-time receptionist job.

Grayson's career acts—After Grayson finished her MBA with combined concentrations in marketing and international business, she went to work in brand management for a prestigious global consumer packaged goods organization. This position is considered an outstanding opportunity and very impressive on the all-important résumé. Once she was in the organization, however, she realized this was not the career she had in mind (despite the fact that she was in the best possible role for someone at her level) because it had her far removed from the cross-cultural work she enjoyed. While in her MBA program, Grayson had already started a second career act: Grayson was drawn to volunteer with the diverse international student population. She audited the class on U.S. culture and business to provide an American student perspective, and delivered cross-cultural counseling and language assistance through an English conversation group with classmates from Japan and Korea. She even volunteered to help the international spouses learn about the United States through the joys of cooking.

After graduate school and while working full time, she continued to build her second career act by learning more about the importance of effective cross-cultural communication in global business and also creating a Web site to help international MBA students and their families learn, succeed, and have fun throughout their U.S. experience. After two years of working in consumer packaged goods, she resigned and dedicated 100% of her time and energy to her cross-cultural consulting business. She shed a less-interesting career act for a more interesting one seamlessly. Within one year, she was making more money with the cross-cultural business, doing what she loves.

The knowledge, skills, and abilities Grayson gained from her volunteer work while still in graduate school set a solid foundation for her cross-cultural business today. Through volunteering to help her fellow students adjust to living and attending school in the United States, she was able to clearly see what was needed from a business perspective and how it could best be delivered. She perfected her career act through volunteer work that was highly fulfilling.

As in Janet and Grayson's cases, there are many ways to squeeze the most out of your starter and progressive career acts:

- Ask for additional roles. Anything that will give you greater knowledge or help build your skills and abilities is useful. If you are very new in your career, additional tasks might help you gain a better sense for the way you like to work.

- Volunteer for tasks that will give you exposure and help you build the knowledge, skills, and abilities you need.

- Seek a mentor who has already made it in your ideal career act.

- Demonstrate your commitment to the industry or field so that others want to help you further your career.

- Be attentive and engaged to gain the most from the experiences you are offered.

Exercise 8 will help you think through ways to close the knowledge, skill, and/or ability gap as you move toward your ideal career act.

Exercise 8: Self-Development to Close the Gap in Knowledge, Skills, and Abilities

• What knowledge, skills, and abilities do I need to move closer to obtaining my ideal career act? _____

_____

• How can I gain the necessary knowledge and build my skills and abilities?

_____

_____

• How will I know if I have gained this knowledge and have reached some level of proficiency with the necessary skills and abilities? _____

_____

_____

Gaining the knowledge, skills, and abilities for any ideal career act might take time. You might have raw talent or natural ability, but your skills will still need to be honed over time. In his book *Outliers: The Story of Success*,[4] Malcolm Gladwell beautifully illustrates this point. He coins a "10,000 hour rule" that seems to be the pattern of many successful and highly talented people from Bill Gates to Wolfgang Amadeus Mozart and the Beatles. Gladwell demonstrates that, while naturally gifted, these individuals invested at least 10,000 hours into honing their talent before realizing their career success noting that "ten thousand hours is the magic number of greatness."

Any starter or progressive career act, when consistent with your plan to move you closer to your ideal career act, will be beneficial—even if it is volunteer experience or a part-time career act. Use these starter career acts as an opportunity to improve and develop your knowledge, skills, and abilities.

It is important to point out that you should plan your exit from these starter career acts as well as you planned your entrance into them. Before beginning a job, try to ascertain what you want out of it and, after achieving the goal, plan for the exit. It has always seemed imbalanced to me that we work hard to enter a job but, once we are in it, allow fate and serendipity to take over. Remember the major theme of this book: You are in control of your own career destiny so you need to chart your course into—and out of—career acts to get closer to having more of what you really want from your life and your career.

chapter four

Enjoy Financial and Professional Security

"You have to perform at a consistently higher level than others. That's the mark of a true professional."
Joe Paterno

Karl Wallenda, the founder and leader of the famous daredevil family of stunt performers known as "The Flying Wallendas," was once quoted as saying that "life is being on the wire, everything else is just waiting."[1] During a high-wire act in 1978, Karl Wallenda fell to his death at age 73. He died, as many have said, doing what he loved. If you have ever seen the high-wire walkers' act, you know they are the stars of the circus: The music builds to underscore the danger of the act they will perform. The audience's trepidation is in the air they breathe. The spotlight shines only on them.

As we have learned from Karl Wallenda's life and death, the high-wire walkers' acts are thrilling—but come with the greatest risks of all acts. If you have a single career act working for an organization, you are a metaphorical career high-wire walker. Just as the high-wire walker is the riskiest act in the circus, in today's employment climate, a single career act is the riskiest way to manage your career.

Risky, however, is not impossible.

In fact, if you are like most Americans, you have a single career act. You work for an employer—small or large. Although I am not an advocate of single career acts, relying on organizations as your only source of employment, I can fully understand that having multiple career acts is not right for everyone or that they might take some time to build.

If you have only one career act and are working for an organization (especially if you only want one career act in the future), seriously consider the advice in this chapter to bolster your professional and financial security while making yourself less susceptible to the next organizational layoff. In addition, many outstanding Web sites offer contemporary advice on how to succeed in the corporate world with an awareness of the new psychological contract. Some examples include the following:

- www.45things.com
- www.CareerAdviceBlogs.com
- www.CareerDiva.net
- www.Careerealism.com
- www.CareerRocketeer.com
- www.JibberJobber.com
- www.JonathanFields.com
- www.LindseyPollak.com
- www.PaulaCaligiuri.com
- www.TheWorkBuzz.com

Creating Financial and Professional Security through Your Organizational Role

To lower the risk of being downsized or fired from any of your career acts, you need to secure your career with a metaphorical safety net. The strength of your safety net in each career act is measured by how critical and how unique you are to your business, employer, team, customers, clients, and others who make decisions about your continued employment. It is a straightforward formula: The more critical and unique your role is, and the greater your excellence in the role, the greater financial and professional security you will have.

You can create more secure career acts within organizations in a variety of ways. The following sections discuss the two that I consider most important.

Occupying a Critical Role

If you are in a support-staff or ancillary role in your organization, you are in the riskiest possible position because you are one of the first to be downsized when organizational cuts are needed. Most organizations manage their human resources well enough to know that the last people they would ever cut in an economic downturn would be those in wealth-creating positions. Employees who are creating high-demand products and services—and those who are effectively selling them—are the most secure.

As we have seen with recent job cuts, professional employees and senior executives are not immune from being downsized. As Drs. Mark Huselid, Dick Beatty, and Brian Becker note in their seminal books and articles,[2] the critical "A" positions are those crucial to a company's ability to execute some part of the company's strategy.

Are you in one of those critical roles? Criticality to the organization is not about the level in the organization. Even well-qualified professionals are encouraged to think carefully about the type of role they select for their career act. For example, a lawyer who is a member of a manufacturing company's legal department would be in a support role (he or she costs the company money). The same lawyer working for a law firm would be in a wealth-creating role (he or she brings in money for the company). Be sure you perform a wealth-creating career act that will be central to the success of your employer.

Being Unique in Your Role

As individuals, every one of us is irreplaceable. We are unique. Unfortunately, in terms of the education, experience, knowledge, skills, and abilities we bring to our employers, some of us are considered more unique than others. If your position is one that could be accomplished by many individuals effectively, you are at greater risk of being downsized than someone who is doing a job very few people could accomplish effectively. Consider your role in the organization: *Are there others who do your job?* Consider the labor market: *How difficult would it be to find your replacement (especially in today's labor market reality)?* Be honest with yourself.

Drs. Dave Lepak and Scott Snell suggest that the most strategic positions within organizations are those highly critical roles held by people who have unique skills.[3] Across your career acts you want to demonstrate your unique skills, ideally performing each of your career acts in a way that would be almost impossible for your employer to replace.

Try to attain a career act that will leverage your unique knowledge, skills, and abilities (and ideally your talents, passions, and interests also). If you do not have a unique set of knowledge, skills, and abilities, consider the way you do your job: *Are there ways you can accomplish your job that brings additional value to the role, but leverages something only you could do?* Let's consider the single-act careers of Venus and Beth. They both occupy critical and unique roles and, at the same time, leverage their talents, passions, and interests.

Venus's career act—Working in a managerial-level government job, Venus felt unfulfilled. She wanted to apply her administrative and public relations skills to serve the greater good. After researching the job market at the time, Venus sought and accepted a job as the public relations liaison for a large, nonprofit organization dedicated to helping children with disabilities. Working for an organization dedicated to such a worthwhile cause was fulfilling her need to care for others. Being a part of the team of those who sought out donations (the lifeblood of this nonprofit) was mission-driven for her. Her role in public relations was a natural fit. Venus has a unique set of abilities: She is perhaps one of the warmest, most loving, and effective communicators I have ever met. Everyone who meets Venus instantly trusts her— and with good reason. She is honest and caring. Venus loves what she does and is clearly in the best possible single career act for her. She has no interest in adding an additional career act.

Beth's career act—Beth had originally thought she would go to law school after completing her bachelor's degree. To test whether the field of law would be interesting before she made the full investment, she decided to first become a paralegal and work for a few years. After completing a paralegal training program, she went to work for a large law firm. The experience was revealing and confirmed that, although she was still interested in the law, she did not like the way lawyers in the large firms worked, especially the hours they worked. She was also bored with the lack of variation in the tasks she was given as a paralegal.

Instead of giving up on the field of law, Beth decided to try a smaller firm, one that was a broad-based practice, one that would give her greater exposure to the different aspects of the law. When she made that change, Beth's level of fulfillment went up. Working as the trusted paralegal for a sole practitioner attorney on interesting and diverse legal cases was fascinating and truly gratifying. Beth conducts legal research, writes briefs, helps with jury selection, and performs tasks to prepare for closings, hearings, and trials. The relationship with her employer is strong and valued; the attorney clearly trusts and appreciates Beth and the outstanding work she does.

Most recently, Beth has been expanding her skill set and has started taking over the accounting for the small law firm, an area she enjoys. The small law firm has begun to hire additional staff, and Beth's single career act is enlarging in more interesting ways. She is indispensible to her employer and loves what she does.

Both Venus and Beth have very different roles but share the similarities for outstanding single career acts. Both are critical to the success of their organizations. Through donations, Venus helps raise the revenue needed for her nonprofit organization. Beth raises revenue for the small law firm by efficiently and effectively providing paralegal services, which are directly billable to the law firm's clients.

Both offer a unique set of skills and abilities. Venus has exemplary interpersonal and organizational skills combined with a personal desire to see her organization succeed that, together, would be difficult to find in another person. Beth brings exceptional commitment and excellence to her work and also has the ability to instill trust in clients and in her employer. In both cases, Venus and Beth have an extraordinary combination of personal and professional skills that would be very difficult to replace.

Creating Financial and Professional Security through Effective Self-Management

As a work psychologist, I have had countless opportunities to interact with people at all organizational levels, some very senior executives and some entry-level or nonprofessional staff. I have career counseled

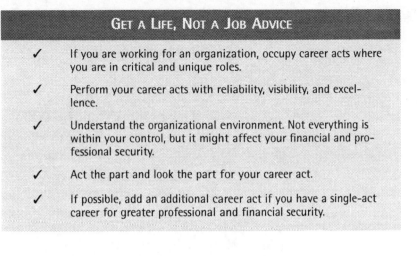

Get a Life, Not a Job Advice

- ✓ If you are working for an organization, occupy career acts where you are in critical and unique roles.
- ✓ Perform your career acts with reliability, visibility, and excellence.
- ✓ Understand the organizational environment. Not everything is within your control, but it might affect your financial and professional security.
- ✓ Act the part and look the part for your career act.
- ✓ If possible, add an additional career act if you have a single-act career for greater professional and financial security.

people from very small and very large organizations. I have observed and worked with those who are wildly successful and some who are one small mistake away from losing their jobs.

One thing I know for sure: Books can never capture the intricacies of what really happens among humans when they work together—and what makes some of them highly successful and others self-destruct. Nevertheless, books and Web sites are valuable. There are hundreds (probably thousands) of books and Web sites proffering career advice. If you work for an organization and you need some advice on how to acquire more critical roles or be more successful in your current one, I suggest you take a trip to your local bookstore or library or visit any of the Web sites suggested in the previous section. When you work for an organization, especially if you opt for a single-act career, you should seek as much sound career advice as you can find.[4]

This book would need to be several volumes long if I tried to cover every piece of relevant advice on how to succeed within organizations. We could have volumes dedicated to how to win promotions,

FIND A MENTOR

I suggest finding a mentor within your organization, ideally someone who will guide you through the idiosyncrasies of the organization because he or she has done this successfully. Your mentor should be someone who is not threatened by you and wants to see you succeed. Your mentor should be someone who takes the time to understand you as a person, your strengths, and your weaknesses. Ideally, your mentor has power and influence within the organization.

Finding a mentor who you trust, with whom you can easily communicate, and who wants to engage in a mentor-mentee relationship with you is not easy, but very valuable and highly developmental. It has been my experience that some of the best mentoring relationships have happened very naturally. The typical scenario is that a junior person consults with a senior person on a task-specific question. The junior person, over time, is respected by the senior person and engages in deeper career-related conversations. Put yourself out there to find a mentor. If you are already very senior, you might need a mentor within your industry (but not your company) or a retired executive you respect. Remember you can use all of the great advice you can find if you are performing a single career act in an organization.

gain power and influence, navigate office politics, and so on. This chapter is not comprehensive, but it does offer some themes from my observations of people on either end of the *"wildly successful"* to *"about to self-destruct"* continuum. The following are three self-management strategies to increase your financial and professional security while working for an organization.

Performing Reliably

Are you the "go-to" person in your work group when things need to be accomplished on a tight deadline or the work is particularly critical? If so, you can skip this section. You are already considered a reliable performer. If you think others are deemed as highly reliable, but you are not, try some of the following suggestions:

- **Reduce your drama around deadlines and other pressured work situations**—Everyone has them. Handle them with grace.

- **Be available**—This does not mean that you should always be the first one in the office every morning and the last one to leave every evening. In fact, in most organizational cultures, this just demonstrates your inefficiency. Rather, if additional work is needed, be available without much fuss.

- **Offer more value than what is requested**—Try to anticipate what else would be useful and if you can provide it effectively, do it. For example, if you are asked to put together a presentation based on some materials, also put together the corresponding speaker's notes, the notes the speaker can use to give his or her presentation. A research student did that for me once and she quickly became my indispensible "go-to" person.

- **Deliver on promises**—"Underpromise and overdeliver" is a popular quote by business guru Tom Peters. In career counseling, I share his quote frequently to help talented and highly motivated professionals positively shape their reputations. Stretch goals are great, and I never want to squelch your motivation, confidence, or optimism; I do, however, want you to consider how promises might affect your professional reputation.

Overpromising (even with the best of intentions) unfortunately damages professional reputations when you fail to deliver—negatively affecting your credibility and the perceptions of your competence. In today's business environment, it is always better to consistently exceed everyone's expectations. (Remember that accolades are not often given for merely meeting expectations, only exceeding them.) Try to balance the following three factors the next time you make a promise on a work-related deliverable:

- **Promises on work products**—It is always a good idea to overdeliver on the quality of your work product, giving your client, supervisor, or colleague more than what he or she expects. Unless there is some perverse professional jealously, overdelivering on the quality of your work will always reflect positively on your credibility and competence.

- **Promises on deadlines**—With respect to deadlines, I offer the opposite advice. Producing something ahead of time can be interpreted negatively—as if you are not expending the appropriate level of effort on the work product. Promise and adhere to the most realistic deadline possible. Deliver when you say you will deliver. If you are finished ahead of time, use the time to improve the quality of the work product.

- **Promises on price or resources**—Managing your promises on price and necessary resources needed for a work product (e.g., materials) is far more nuanced. If you come in under expectations, you might be appreciated temporarily (provided the quality is high); however, keep in mind that you have permanently set your bar lower for future projects. In most circumstances, it is better to charge what is expected or use the resources in a way that is consistent with those expectations. The positive benefit of coming in underbudget or using fewer resources is never as great as you would expect because the resources were already committed. The opposite is far worse: Damage to your reputation can be high if you need to ask a client or supervisor for more money or more resources to complete the project.

Deciding what to promise and what to deliver is an art in the professional world and important for protecting your reputation as a reliable person in a career act.

Performing Visibly

Make sure people can see your career act. Your uniqueness might not be noticed if your contributions are hidden, your role is not visible, or if you don't take credit when it is due to you. If you rarely receive direct feedback on your contribution, that is a good indication that your contribution might not be visible. *Who in your organization knows what you do?* Only you can determine the best way to gain more visibility appropriately, without appearing pushy, threatening, or arrogant.

Many times, getting more visibility is as simple as just asking your supervisor for some visibility. You could try asking something like: *"Do you think I might be able to sit in on the meeting when you present the designs to the client? I am curious to see their reaction, and it will help me learn how to give client presentations myself in the future."* Or possibly: *"Would I be able to attend one of your weekly update meetings? I'd like to learn more about how you connect the dots with the other units. It would help me better understand our business."* If your supervisor says "no" without a plausible reason, then he or she is likely feeling threatened by you—which means that you have a bigger problem with your single career act for as long as he or she remains your supervisor. (Sorry, this is tough love. I want to see you happy. An unsupportive supervisor should signal to you that this career act is probably not going to end well.)

The flip side of this problem (and one much easier to fix) is to accept the credit you deserve. This suggestion is for those who value modesty and humility to a fault. Some people need no advice on professional boasting, and I am not trying to create more organizational egomaniacs. But I am encouraging you to be proud of the excellent work you do. *Do you find it difficult to use the phrase "I did..." and prefer to say "we did..." even when you acted solo?* If so, this piece of advice is for you. Start small: When someone compliments you, simply say "thank you" and nothing else. If a colleague says, "I like your new briefcase," say "thank you." If a colleague says, "that was a great report," say "thank you." If you are modest to a fault, this will not be easy. Practice. Once you get over your discomfort with accepting compliments, you can start to work your way up to talking about your accomplishments and comfortably receiving credit for what you do well.

Performing with Excellence

In most organizational environments, this means that you execute your tasks with excellence. The best evidence of your performance should be others' response to your work product, such as compliments, criticisms, and performance reviews. I would not suggest waiting for an annual performance review to make sure you are performing your career act with excellence. Make a habit of asking your supervisor and other trusted colleagues for suggestions, honest feedback on ways to improve your career act.

Performing with excellence might mean putting in extra effort if you are not 100% ready for your career act. You might need to practice a presentation at home in front of your spouse or a mirror. You might need to do some research work at home to perfect your presentation or report. The possibilities to help you execute your visible roles flawlessly are as varied as the jobs that exist. The bottom line is to be great at what you do—whatever it is.

If you occupy (or want to occupy) a single career act, I strongly encourage you to take some time to work through Exercise 9 for your job in the organization where you are currently. You can also use the exercise to diagnose what might have gone wrong at an organization you left in the past. In this exercise, you are asked to honestly assess your career act's CURVE:

Criticality

Uniqueness

Reliability

Visibility

Excellence

Exercise 9: Assessing Your CURVE (criticality, uniqueness, Reliability, visibility, and Excellence)

Instructions: Give yourself 1 point for each "yes." You can have a maximum of 3 points for each set of questions and a maximum total of 15 points overall.

Criticality Score:

1. Are you integral for the success of your organization?

2. Does your work directly influence the bottom line of your organization?

3. Would your organization be less competitive and effective if you left?

Uniqueness Score:

1. Are you the only person who can perform your job effectively?

2. If you left the organization, would it take months (and not weeks) to find your replacement?

3. Is your combination of skills considered rare in the labor market?

Reliability Score:

1. Are you the person everyone goes to with critical tasks?

2. Are you the person people trust to deliver reliably what you promise?

3. Are you the person everyone knows is willing to put in extra effort when needed?

Visibility Score:

1. Do many people know the contribution you make in your organization?

2. Does your supervisor give you opportunities for visibility among senior leaders?

3. Do many people in the organization know you personally?

Excellence Score:

1. Are you regularly complimented on your work product?

2. Do you receive the best possible performance review scores or evaluations?

3. Are you considered one of the best in your organization for the role you are in?

Working for Organizations: Looking the Part and Acting the Part

If you want a career act with an organization (especially a single-act career), you might need to align with the company-specific norms for style, communication, and professional behaviors. Whether we like it or not, organizations have cultures, and your ability to fit in with the culture might affect your ability to succeed in it. Often, the nuances of a corporate culture are unspoken—for example, there might not be a policy against earrings for male employees, but you might observe that the males who wear earrings are not the ones given the first opportunity for promotion.

I don't like saying this because I strongly believe in individual expression, which is part of the reason I rally against an overreliance on a single employer. However, if you want to work in an organization, and increase your financial and professional security, there are some rules. In the best case, you already share organizational values and norms, so it will not feel disingenuous.

(Sigh) here goes: There are many overt symbols that might affect whether you are perceived as being a person who fits in:

- The quality and style of your clothes
- How well you are groomed or "pulled together" (your haircut, accessories, makeup for women)
- Your office, cubicle, or workspace décor (toys, photos, artwork)
- Your communication style

In some workplace cultures, these seemingly superficial things matter and in others, no one cares about them in the slightest. You need to assess this for yourself by observing those who are successful. Take a careful look at the people in various levels of the organization. *Do you sense that the higher you look in the organization, the more homogeneous they are in terms of what they wear, how they act, how they communicate, and the like?*[5] If the answer is "yes," try to note what is similar among them. *Do you value what they seem to value?* Only if your honest answer is "yes" should you conform for the sake of a career act.

If you do not share the values you see at the top of the organization, conforming might lead to a promotion, but it will not lead to your fulfillment. In that case, you might want to find a different company for your single career act. Please see the sidebar, "A Note about

Discrimination and Homogeneity in the Workforce," for additional comments about homogeneity and discrimination and Exercise 10 for a method for assessing your path for future success within a single organization.

A NOTE ABOUT DISCRIMINATION AND HOMOGENEITY IN THE WORKFORCE

There is a difference between "looking the part" and "acting the part"—and discrimination in terms of race, gender, and so on. If you are a woman, for example, and see no other women in senior levels of your organization, you need to assess the situation carefully and realistically. Do you believe there is a glass ceiling (one that will keep you from moving ahead to the career act you want) caused by either subtle or overt gender discrimination? Or, is it the case that high-performing women are promoted proportionally to the number available in the talent pipeline (that is, group of people from whom promotions are made)? It might be the case that there are a low number of women in the talent pipeline from the very start, causing fewer to be represented at the top levels in the organization.

In most well-managed organizations, at least the ones for which you would want to work, it is the latter. Well-managed organizations (both small and large) will *value people* and the contributions they make. They will not discriminate on the basis of race, gender, and so on because they would view not leveraging their entire pool of talent as a competitive disadvantage.

If you sense there is real discrimination (and not a function of the number of any given minority group in the talent pipeline), please look for a better opportunity elsewhere first— and then leave that organization. *You deserve to be in career acts where you will be appreciated, valued, and rewarded.*

A Note if You Want to Be on a Managerial Track within the Organization

Even at the most senior levels of organizations, I have watched numerous technically excellent managers derail before reaching the executive suite because they were deemed to not have "executive presence." I cannot think of a more frustrating piece of feedback to give bright, competent managers than to tell them "they lack executive presence" without clarity on what is meant by the phrase.

In some cases, the "lack of executive presence" is behavioral and we can correct it with relative ease through training or coaching. The managers, in these cases, usually need to clean up their performances, so to speak. They need to change some behavior that is sending the wrong message to those who are making promotion decisions. The five most common are as follows:

- **Disorganized work area or messy office**—These send the unintentional message that the person is doing slipshod work. The remedy, a bit of training on organizational skills and neatness, is an easy fix. In the spirit of honesty, I have to confess that my university office is really a mess. I can get away with this in the academic setting, keeping in mind that the phrase "absentminded professor" has a nice (or tolerated) ring to it. My office has not held me back in any way. But in some organizations, it would.

- **Sloppy appearance**—Much like the office, a person's sloppy appearance might be giving the same impression as the messy office and can generally be corrected with some conversations about style and grooming.

- **Poor manners**—Poor manners are often at the root of why certain people are not promoted in some organizations: Those in control of promotions do not promote those who don't play well in the sandbox. (It is their sandbox, after all.) If this problem is behavioral and they want to improve in this area, coaching can involve some role playing or training on active listening, etiquette, and positive communication.

- **Poor communications**—I have seen many brilliant people be unable to reach their next desired level in their career act because they are unable to effectively communicate their thoughts (usually verbally). The solution generally involves coaching on verbal communication, public speaking, and presentation skills.

- **Lack of confidence**—Other technically gifted people are stifled in their career acts because of their own timidity. Whether real or perceived, they give the sense to others that they are unsure about their work, opinions, and decisions. These individuals can work on their ability to exude vibes of confidence, to present themselves as a person in control. This can be achieved through improving verbal skills and learning to present oneself assertively with other small behavioral changes, such as posture and eye contact.

In other cases, especially when applied to people who will be leading other people, "executive presence" is somewhat more dispositional and, as a result, more difficult to change through coaching or training. To be promoted, an individual needs to be seen as a "leader" in the eyes of those making the promotion decisions because he or she will need to provide vision and motivate others to follow. When given more vague feedback about their "lack of executive presence" (and none of the five from the preceding list seem to apply), we usually need to work on helping the person find his or her "center for attraction"—the thing that makes people want to follow him or her.

Identifying a center for attraction and developing it is far more difficult to coach because it is generally a function of the person's natural charm, charisma, extroversion, ease with others, and other qualities that are difficult to quantify. In some cases, honestly, this cannot be changed or developed. Some individuals remain brilliant in their technical or functional areas, but are not deemed to be leaders within their chosen organization. They might be wonderful leaders in another organization or context, but the decision makers in the current organization are not recognizing their ability to be promoted.

If you desire an ideal career act in an organization where you believe executive presence might matter, you might want to look for ways to perform so that others can easily visualize you in the role. The changes, if you are honest with yourself about the behaviors that need to be altered, might be relatively straightforward. *The big question is whether you want to change for the sake of the career act.* If the answer is "no," you should find a career act where you will be appreciated and rewarded for being exactly who you want to be, wearing what you want to wear, grooming as you want to groom, and so on. *You see the pattern, right?* A multiple-act career (even with a single career act) is all about you and what you, not your employer, find fulfilling about the way you work.

Exercise 10: Assessing Your Path for Promotion in Your Career Act

Spend some time (you might need a few months to do this exercise effectively) observing selected people within three different levels above you in your organization (if your organization has that many levels). Complete the following table as thoroughly as possible.

For reasons that I hope are obvious, my strong recommendation is that you complete this exercise at home, not at work where others might see it.

Level and Names	Observe the Individuals' Names in Column 1 and Answer the Following Questions:		
Column 1	Column 2	Column 3	Column 4
Level 1—Name three people at the highest level in your organization 1. 2. 3.	What are the five most salient behaviors, attitudes, values, knowledge, skills, or abilities consistent among these three individuals? 1. 2. 3. 4. 5.	How are their behaviors, attitudes, values, knowledge, skills, or abilities different from the three people in Level 2?	
Level 2—Name three people who are one or two levels below the highest level (but above you) in your organization 1. 2. 3.	What are the five most salient behaviors, attitudes, values, knowledge, skills, or abilities consistent among these individuals? 1. 2. 3. 4. 5.	How are their behaviors, attitudes, values, knowledge, skills, or abilities different from the three people in Level 3?	What changes would these individuals need to make to be promoted to Level 1?

Level and Names	Observe the Individuals' Names in Column 1 and Answer the Following Questions:		
Column 1	Column 2	Column 3	Column 4
Level 3—Name three people who are above you but below those in Level 2 1. 2. 3.	What are the five most salient behaviors, atti-tudes, values, knowledge, skills, or abilities consis-tent among these individuals? 1. 2. 3. 4. 5.		What changes would these three individuals need to make to be pro-moted to Level 2?

Now, let's analyze you and your potential career act with this organization.

Review the lists in the second and third columns of the table.

1. Circle all of the behaviors, attitudes, values, knowledge, skills, or abilities you already have.

2. Now star the behavioral, attitudinal, or values-based changes you would like to (or be happy to) make. Also star the knowledge, skills, and abili-ties you would like to gain. Be honest with yourself. There are no right or wrong answers. You need to stay true to yourself to assess whether this organization is the right place for your career act.

Review the lists in the fourth column, relative to your preceding answers.

1. Would you be interested in making the type of behavioral, attitudinal, or values-based changes you have identified in Column 4, if you were required to do so?

2. Would you be interested in gaining the knowledge, skills, and abilities you have just identified, if the same changes were required of you? Do you believe you will be able to do this?

Summary

1. Based on this quick analysis, making all of the changes you want to make, what is the highest level you could likely achieve?

2. Is this the level of your ideal career act? What does this exercise tell you about yourself and your potential for success for a single career act with this organization?

Understanding How Organizational Culture and Politics Will Affect Your Professional and Financial Security

Within organizations of all sizes, there are political games and shifts in power. No matter how critical, unique, reliable, visible, and excellent you are, you might fall victim to organizational changes beyond your control, such as mergers, acquisitions, reorganizations, and divestitures. Even a change of personnel in a level above you might result in a personality clash or simply the loss of a supportive supervisor. These are to be expected when working for an organization. Keep your ear to the ground to learn what is happening before it is formally announced in your organization.

Office or organizational politics produce more challenging shifts to the environment because they are less obvious to those who are not pulling the political strings. Political alliances often form when people try to gain power through their networks, creating in-groups and out-groups among employees. Regardless of whether you know this is happening, you might find yourself aligned with the wrong group when the political wind shifts. This is unfortunate for those who are swept along unsuspectingly because they did not realize they were being co-opted into a political alliance in the first place. Regardless of how you feel about office politics, it behooves you to understand the politics of your office or organization.

To navigate through the shifting winds of office politics, try to work effectively across multiple organizational groups (including divisions, levels, or functional areas). Be a person who understands the political dynamics but does not play them if it can be avoided. I never feel sorry for those who obviously try too hard to play politics—those who use their shifting alliances, rather than their personal competence, to get ahead. (I like the term "toxically political" for this type of behavior.) At the other extreme, I do feel sorry for those who are oblivious to the fact that politics exist. But be aware: Both ends of this continuum usually run into trouble at some point in their organizational career acts. The following are a few pieces of advice about organizational politics:

- **Do not be blind to office politics**—They exist everywhere; some places are more political than others but there will always be alliances among people and shifts in power and influence.

- **Understand organizational politics without being toxically political yourself**—If you ignore politics completely, you will be viewed as naïve. It is fine to acknowledge them, even leverage them, without making the organizational culture more closed or uncomfortable. In the most painfully political places, knowledge is hoarded and shared sparingly with only the right people. If you are doing that, you are part of the problem.

- **Try to anticipate the political changes that are happening within your business and stay ahead of the curve**—Just as the tightrope walker about to step on the banana peel, you don't want to miss a change coming in your environment. Listen. Talk to your mentor. Ask questions.

Try to get some confirmation from multiple reliable sources.

■ **Know how you are perceived with respect to political alliances**—I've seen very senior managers and outstanding performers fired because they were part of a political alliance which, for whatever reason, fell out of favor politically and lost power. This scenario is less upsetting when politics were played and the winds shifted—and far more upsetting when apolitical people are perceived to be aligned, without intention or knowledge because they shared an interest (for example, ran together at lunch) and had become friends outside of work.

Assessing the Level of Security in Your Organization-Based Career Act

We know that the single career act is the riskiest, especially now when companies are going through downsizing in an effort to remain competitive. The high unemployment rate has heightened everyone's anxiety, but we need to remember that not everyone should be concerned.

How do you know whether your job is at risk? There are three factors to consider when determining whether you are at risk of losing your job: your organization's stability, the criticality and uniqueness of your role, and your job performance in your role. You can assess these in Exercise 11. This tool is also available online at www. PaulaCaligiuri.com.

Exercise 11: Assessing Your Risk for Losing Your Job

Risk Factor #1: Assess Your **Organization's Stability**

Check all of the following you have observed:

- ☐   There is a hiring freeze.

- ☐   There is a freeze on nonessential travel.

- ☐   Open positions are not being filled.

- ☐   Temporary contracts are not being renewed.

- ☐   Your company was recently acquired.

If you have more than two of these checked, your organization's stability is a risk factor.

Risk Factor #2: Assess Your **Role**

Check all of the following that seem to describe your role:

- ☐   I am in a support role, as opposed to a line role.

- ☐   My role does not directly create wealth for the organization.

- ☐   The company could still be competitive, even without someone in my role.

- ☐   My skills are relatively easy to find in the labor market.

- ☐   I could be easily replaced internally.

If you have more than two of these checked, your role is a risk factor.

Risk Factor #3: Assess Your **Job Performance**

Check all of the following that seem to describe your job performance:

☐ My most recent performance rating was less than perfect.

☐ I am occasionally late for work.

☐ My work is occasionally criticized.

☐ There are better-performing employees holding my same job title.

☐ Some people would say I am a difficult person to work with.

If you have more than two of these checked, your job performance is a risk factor.

How Many of the Three Risk Factors Do You Have?

If you have no risk factors, the likelihood that you will lose your job is probably low. Revisit this periodically to assess whether the situation has changed.

If you have one risk factor, there is some risk that you might lose your job. If you like your organization and your only risk factor is your role, you might want to consider whether there is a more central or core position in your organization where your skills can be applied. The more you are in a critical role, the safer your job. Likewise, you might want to gain additional high-demand skills as the additional skills will make you more difficult to replace. The risk factor over which you have the greatest control is your job performance. If this is a concern, you might want to recommit yourself to performing reliably and with excellence in your role.

If you have two or three risk factors, you have some reason to be concerned. You might want to proactively begin to look for another job while you still have one.

Adding a Career Act to Increase Professional and Financial Security

I hope Exercise 11 did not add to your stress level. This is not my goal—I promise. Nonetheless, while I am worried about raising your stress level, I need to share some issues about stress as they relate to single-act careers. Work-related stress is caused, in part, when employees lack control over their resources, how they work, how they allocate their time, and the like.

Single-act careers can be particularly stressful because much of your professional resources are being controlled by your organization. The cover of *Fortune Magazine's* November 2005 issue was dedicated to the stress and burnout of the most elite group of executive-level employees within organizations. In this issue, senior executives were surveyed about their issues of work-life balance. Although 49% of the respondents were self-described workaholics, 64% stated that at this stage of their life they would choose more time over money. These statistics are very revealing, given that these are the individuals who tend to be perceived as having the "best" jobs within an organization. They have money but not time—and long for more time.

I am not suggesting that financial freedom is not important. It is a career goal that comes with successful careers. For your peace of mind and security, financial freedom is critical. I do believe, however, that financial freedom should not be achieved at the expense of your work-life balance.

A world-renowned psychologist once told me in jest, *"I remember when I had a lot of time but no money. I now have a lot of money but no time. I believe there was a day in between."* Actually, this psychologist has an amazing career and a tremendous amount of flexibility to enjoy both his time and his money. His point, however, is well taken. We should not need to sacrifice time for money to achieve financial flexibility. We should also not need to sacrifice money for time to achieve work-life balance.

Having more control over your multiple career acts will give you the flexibility to balance your time but also some security to not rely on any one career act. I end this chapter the same way I started it—by reminding you that the riskiest of all career acts is the single career act, with the organization being your only income-generating activity. If you have an outside interest, passion, hobby, or talent, please explore the possibility of adding an additional career act.

chapter five

Increase Your Mental, Physical, and Emotional Well-Being

"The first requisite of success is the ability to apply your physical and mental energies to one problem without growing weary."

Thomas Edison

Before planning and coordinating your multiple career acts, take a look inward. *Are you in the best possible place—mentally, physically, and emotionally—to manage your multiple career acts?* Doing what you love is stimulating and fulfilling; however, if you embed multiple career acts into an anxiety-filled or low-energy lifestyle, you will be setting yourself up for great personal frustration. The increased demands of multiple career acts require increased stamina and greater emotional strength.

You can prepare for a multiple-act career by focusing on your physical health and your emotional well-being. You don't need to live on this earth for very long to know they are all related. Emotions affect your physical health and vice versa. Use this section like a computer's virus checker for your life's system. Give your life system a scan to see what habits need to be rebooted (or perhaps just booted) to prepare for a multiple-act career.

Improving Your Mental, Physical, and Emotional Well-Being to Improve Your Career Acts

To manage the demands of a multiple-act career, especially at the onset, individuals need their physical health, energy, stamina, and emotional well-being to keep up with the demands of multiple career acts.

In the sphere of physical health, I am not an expert. I am neither a physician nor a nutritionist. I am a work psychologist who has had the opportunity to speak with hundreds of people about what they do for a living. From the overt appearances of health (such as weight, skin tone, and energy level), I have observed that those who are fulfilled in their careers are also healthier. In fact, unintentionally (but not coincidentally), everyone profiled in this book is fit and healthy.

It probably will not surprise you to know that the *Journal of Occupational and Environmental Medicine* cites health-care expenditures nearly 50% greater for workers who report high stress levels, so by reducing the level of occupational stress, companies benefit from significantly decreased health-care expenses. Regarding absenteeism,

GET A LIFE, NOT A JOB ADVICE

✓ Remember all the things your parents taught you about good health: Eat well, get enough sleep, and exercise.

✓ Seek volunteer opportunities where you can improve your career act and experience the energy-giving helper's high.

✓ Take a vacation. The downtime can increase your energy, creativity, and productivity.

✓ Reduce your work-related cynicism through more positive energy. If a career act is really not fulfilling, it is time to look for another career act.

the U.S. Bureau of Labor Statistics found that a median of 25 days away from work occur because of occupational stress, which is over four times the median absence for all injuries and illnesses.

Similarly, in a meta-analysis (a summary of many studies on the same topic) of almost 500 studies covering almost 250,000 people examining the relationship between job satisfaction and health, Drs. Faragher, Cass, and Cooper found positive relationships between job satisfaction and many indicators of health, both physical and psychological.[1]

As you probably know if you have ever taken a statistics course, correlation does not prove causation—that is, people who are satisfied with their jobs are also healthier, but this correlation does not indicate whether good health causes job satisfaction, job satisfaction causes good health, or whether the two are caused by some other factor. Nevertheless, I pose the question: *Which do you think comes first, job satisfaction or physical health?* As a social scientist, I am curious about the causality of the relationship. As a person who cares about individuals' fulfillment, it really does not matter: Career satisfaction, physical health, and psychological health are all useful goals, no matter which comes first.

At the risk of sounding like I am offering a list of New Year's resolutions, you can increase your mental, physical, and emotional well-being to increase your energy and stamina in many ways. Let's consider a few.

Eat Well

Nutritional advice abounds on how to eat a healthy diet. Most of this advice seems to recommend eating foods lower in fat, more lean protein, and moderate natural complex carbohydrates (e.g., whole-wheat bread) instead of simple sugars (e.g., candy). You can do a Web search relatively easily on sites such as the Mayo Clinic or the USDA to receive more than enough advice on eating well.

For the sake of your health, and especially your energy level, it is helpful to eliminate foods that are chemically designed to create the cravings for fat and simple sugars, which is what fast food and junk food do. These foods are designed to be tasty but, in the end, do not help your emotional, mental, or physical health. Think of all of the nutritional pieces of advice you have probably heard in the past: Breakfast is the most important meal of the day. Eat a balanced diet. Eat in moderation. Don't skip meals. Select healthy snacks, such as fruit and nuts. These are relevant pieces of advice and are important for preserving your health.

It is important to mention that many of the people profiled in this book eat organic, locally grown food. They have a healthy relationship with the food and are careful about what foods they put into their bodies. Many are also "foodies," people who love to cook for themselves and also appreciate fine dining. They have both the time and the money to enjoy both activities, clearly an added benefit of multiple career acts.

Exercise

The scientific evidence extolling the benefits of exercise is pervasive. We know that any activity that gets our bodies moving is helpful to our health, energy, and stamina in some way. Even nonexercise activity, such as getting out of your chair every 15 minutes when doing office work, can help maintain a basic level of fitness.[2] Aerobic exercise improves stamina and helps reduce the feelings of mild depression and anxiety. It releases endorphins and gives us a natural high. Strength training and overall fitness increases our metabolism and physical health. *What do you enjoy that will get you moving?*

To stay committed to physical fitness, try to find some activity that you can share with your spouse or a close friend, such as taking brisk walks, playing tennis, or joining a salsa dance class. If you prefer to exercise alone, think about listening to music you find motivating and stimulating. The positive benefits of music are very helpful. You do not need to do much exercise to benefit from the increase in energy. If you have a completely sedentary life, start your exercise regimen with manageable physical activities and, of course, speak with your doctor before starting any exercise.

It follows (and again will not surprise you) that, among those people profiled in this book, there are triathletes, marathon runners, and many who take athletic vacations such as riding bikes through Tuscany, white-water rafting in Colorado, and trips to Tanzania to climb Mount Kilimanjaro. Because they have great careers, they have the time and the money to engage in these activities. Their energy levels and physical fitness makes them healthy and happy with their career acts. It is a virtuous cycle and I want you to experience it.

The following sections describe a few more things you can do to improve your mental, physical, and emotional health.

Improve the Quantity and Quality of Sleep

The Center for Disease Control's National Center for Chronic Disease Prevention and Health Promotion released a report estimating that 50 to 70 million Americans suffer from chronic sleep loss and sleep disorders. Dr. McKnight-Eily reported that sleep loss is associated with health problems, including obesity, depression, and certain risk behaviors, including cigarette smoking, physical inactivity, and heavy drinking.[3] Another sleep expert, psychologist James B. Maas, has found that quality sleep is necessary for peak performance in mental functions, including concentration, memory, critical and creative decision making; leadership functions such as persuasive communication and sustained productivity; and activities requiring coordination such as sports and driving a car.[4]

How many hours of sleep do you average each night? According to the National Sleep Foundation, most adults need between 7 and 9 consecutive hours of sleep each night to feel fully rested. *Are you close to getting the sleep you need?* If not, think of some changes you can make in your daily routine so that you get to bed at the same time every day to get your body into a regular sleep pattern. Avoid stimulants such as coffee, tea, and cola after midday—and be aware that "decaffeinated" coffee still contains some caffeine.

Try to clear your mind before you go to bed; if you tend to lie awake in bed thinking of things you need to do the next day, write them down before "lights out." If reading or TV viewing helps you relax before sleep, make it part of your nightly routine and limit the time so you don't become engrossed, staying up later than you planned. Make sure your bedroom is dark so the light does not wake you, simulating sunlight's cue that it is time to wake up. And try to avoid using your bed for nonsleep activities like paying bills, sending e-mails, or phone conversations. Some bedroom-related nonsleep activities are more than acceptable and, in fact, are great for your well-being.

Laugh. Smile. Have Warm and Fuzzy Feelings.

Do you remember the last time you laughed so hard you cried? Do you remember the feeling immediately after that hearty laugh? It was a natural high, a burst of positive energy, a wonderful buzz. According to Dr. Lee Berk, laughter increases our level of health-enhancing beta-endorphins[5] and this physiological boost lasts about 24 hours after the laughter subsides. Endorphins are neurotransmitters found in the brain that act as the body's own morphine that also influence physiological states, such as our feelings of euphoria.

Volunteer

In addition to laughing, you can also get this natural healthy energy-producing buzz in other ways. Either volunteering your time to a worthy cause (walking dogs for your local animal shelter) or offering a simple act of kindness (helping an elderly person carry his or her groceries) can produce positive health benefits. Think about how you feel when you do nice things for others, especially strangers. You feel good, warm, and fuzzy inside. Psychologists call this feeling the "helper's high." When you do nice things for others and feel the "helper's high," endorphins are released, resulting in positive physical and emotional health benefits. You can channel the euphoria and energy you feel to benefit your life in many ways, such as giving you more energy for your career.

Volunteering has an additional benefit related to improving your career acts. Many acts of volunteerism can, in fact, be starter career acts. These acts of volunteerism, when career-related, offer the coveted "triple win":

- **Win 1**—Society benefits from your time and talents applied to those who are in need.
- **Win 2**—Your health and energy level improves from the helper's high you feel.
- **Win 3**—Your career improves from the opportunity to engage in a starter career act, a way to increase your knowledge, skills, and abilities.

If you are thinking about volunteering, select your volunteerism opportunity carefully. Think about where you can best apply your natural gifts and talents to maximize the benefit to the recipients and increase your helper's high. It is OK that you combine volunteerism with your passions or interests. It is OK that your volunteerism is providing an opportunity to practice a skill. Remember, everyone wins. Let's consider Sue's career acts:

Sue's career acts—Sue has worked as an accountant for years and enjoys her job. When she was in college, she worked as a tutor for an undergraduate accounting class. That experience of tutoring made her realize that she enjoyed teaching, and in the back of her mind she continued to think it might be a fulfilling career. When her daughter began kindergarten, she decided to volunteer every other week to read to the kindergarten children. This act of volunteerism gave her a chance to be closer to her daughter and meet her daughter's teachers and the other parents—but also had the added benefit of fulfilling a curiosity about the possibility of becoming an elementary school teacher in the future.

Everyone wins in Sue's example. By volunteering as a starter career act, she was able to gain knowledge, skills, and abilities. At the same time, her volunteer work gave her an increase in the energy she would need to move into a fulfilling multiple-act career.

Consider Exercise 12 as a way to select the types of volunteer activities that would leverage your time and talents in the best possible way and, at the same time, increase your energy-giving buzz and your knowledge, skills, and abilities.

Take Time Off

Where will you be vacationing this year? Perhaps the better question is: *Will you be taking any vacation at all?* If you are like many Americans, you might be thinking about shortening (or skipping altogether) your vacation this year. A 2008 survey by Expedia.com found that over one third of (already vacation-starved) Americans will not take all of the annual vacation days to which they are entitled.[6]

Many of us cite career-related reasons to forgo our vacations: "I'm too busy and will have too much work when I return." "I'm too critical to be away from the office." "I am worried about being 'out of sight'—especially now when jobs are being cut." *Do any of these*

Exercise 12: Volunteering as a Starter Career Act

1. What do you enjoy as an interest, hobby, or passion (e.g., music, sports, food)?

_____

_____

2. What would you like to explore as a starter career act? _____

_____

_____

3. What knowledge, skills, abilities, occupation areas, or talents do you have (e.g., managerial skills, accounting, graphic design)? _____

_____

_____

4. Thinking creatively, how could your answers to questions 1, 2, and 3 be combined and leveraged in a volunteer setting (e.g., develop and maintain a Web site for the local SPCA to help the animals be adopted, organize the logistics for a local meal-delivery service)? _____

_____

_____

5 Make the call. Set up the meeting. Offer a small amount of your time to start.

_____

_____

_____

sound familiar? Although it is true that there are better and worse times to take vacations for your career, you might be doing more harm to your career by not taking time off to recharge your batteries. We are not machines built to run nonstop.

In fact, a little downtime can actually boost your productivity as vacations (lasting one week or more) have been shown to increase work performance. A recent study, conducted by Air New Zealand in conjunction with former NASA scientists, found that individuals' post-vacation performance improved nearly 25% compared with perform-ance before vacation. The results were even more pronounced for those who likely occupy more senior positions, people 45 years of age and older—demonstrating a 50% increase in their postvacation per-formance.[7]

To maintain peak performance, increase creativity, and improve mental health and physical well-being, vacations are critical. In today's generally overcharged, overly available, ever-changing, and under-staffed organizations, employees run the risk of prolonged exposure to stressful work environments—otherwise known as the recipe for burnout. Given that *performance* is a more important career metric than *attendance* (especially when both can be achieved by simply using the vacation days offered)—and given that the ill effects of burnout can be permanent—even the most career-minded individu-als should consider reaching for the sunblock and trading in some fre-quent flyer miles.

Many companies, realizing the downside of prolonged periods of nonstop work, are encouraging employees to use their vacations by creating *disincentives* to skip vacation—limiting the amount of pay for unused vacation days, limiting the number of days that can be carried over to the next year, rewarding supervisors for encouraging vacations, and the like. Great organizations and great leaders know the positive benefits of employees' vacations.

Let's revisit the possible oppositions standing in the way of your much-deserved vacations:

- **I'm too busy and I'll have too much work when I return**—Many jobs go through annual demand cycles: accountants during tax time, tuxedo renters in the spring and summer, teachers in September, and so on. Try to syn-chronize your vacations to your organization's business cycle, and plan a vacation during an anticipated lighter-workload period. Try to find a coworker to take over the most critical tasks for you so you do not return to an organizational crisis. Give your contact information to your designee so that he or she can contact you if a real work-related emergency arises. Discuss ahead of time what a real emergency is and what can wait, especially if your designee is someone more junior. This is also where I am obligated to advise you to leave your BlackBerry at home and vacation in Wi-Fi dead zones. Realistically, if you are in a very critical role in your organization, being *minimally* connected while on vacation can help reduce your anxiety and any possible feelings of guilt for relaxing while others work. Keep the positive in mind: Your minimally tethered absence is a great way to develop those you supervise, increasing their capability to handle tasks and decisions independently.

- **I'm too critical to be away from the office**—If you are sincerely more concerned about your organizational health over your own, perhaps you should rethink the functional role of vacations in organizational productivity. From a purely competitive perspective, the most critical people in organizations are the very people who tend to be most susceptible to burnout because they seek high-responsibility positions, tend to personalize work, and tend to weave their careers deeply into their self-identity. If this describes you, then a vacation, when well-timed and well-planned, will help *improve* your work performance. Perhaps your more honest psychological concern is that the organization will do just fine without you. If this is the case, look within yourself and build some professional self-confidence.

- **I am worried about being "out of sight"—especially now when jobs are being cut**—This is a reasonable concern, but not realistic for most. Yes, it is true that many organizations are downsizing. However, it is also true that it

121

makes good business sense for organizations to retain those who *consistently perform critical and unique roles exceptionally well*. Moreover, if you are on a list of workers to be laid off, it's unlikely that giving up earned and appropriately timed vacation days would save you from the axe anyway. Vacations and performance excellence are not mutually exclusive, and the more enlightened organizations know that their best performers will burn out if they forsake work-life balance to become martyrs.

If your organization is going through an exceptionally difficult period when taking vacation time is truly impossible, think about taking a minivacation or work-free long weekend. Although the positive effects of vacations are generally associated with longer vacations (at least one week), minivacations will help you decompress. Vacations do not need to require a passport or Platinum Card—just quality time away from thinking about work. For me, a BlackBerry-free week of backyard barbecues, with a few good books, at our lake house is just what the doctor—and career coach—ordered.

Reduce Work-Related Cynicism

Occasional work-related grousing among supportive coworkers or friends during happy hour might not be the best coping mechanism available, but it is *not* work-related cynicism. *Work-related cynicism* is *persistent* and *generalized* and includes feelings of frustration, distrust, negativity, and pessimism about many elements of your work situation (for example, organization, leadership, coworkers, clients, the job itself). Cynicism, along with emotional exhaustion and reduced professional efficacy, are indicators of burnout. Burnout is an extreme form of work-related stress negatively affecting your physical, emotional, and mental well-being. The antidote for burnout, in most cases, is completely changing the work situation, occupation, and so on. Try these five methods for reducing your career-related cynicism before it can become more serious:

1. **Find greater meaning in the work you do.** If you work for an organization, many companies are organizing opportunities for time and effort-based volunteerism. Join in. This will help you connect your company and yourself with the activity of working for a greater good. If you work for yourself or if your company does not offer volunteer opportunities, independently find a volunteer situation where you can lend your professional skills or talents for a greater good. Don't forget, you will also benefit from the helper's high.

2. **If you are working at an organization, try to gain some control over your workload.** It is helpful to say "no" when appropriate and be more assertive if you feel as though you are being treated unfairly in terms of work allocation. If you are performing well, you tend to be rewarded with more work. If you are performing well, you are already valued so suggesting ways for a more equitable distribution of tasks will not reflect negatively on your contribution or effort. You are setting boundaries and gaining control of your situation, which is viewed positively by most people.

3. **Spend more time with colleagues and friends who are positive and supportive**—while avoiding coworkers who are chronic complainers. You might be surprised to learn how profoundly the affect of your coworkers will influence your own mood and energy level.

4. **Try to see "good" in your supervisor, company, coworkers, clients, and so on.** Some people are wired to be more negative and pessimistic. If you have this tendency, try to consciously shape your own behaviors by forcing yourself to observe the positives in the workplace. It might seem contrived, but, over time, it might help shape your cynical attitudes.

5. **Leave.** If your work situation is truly toxic, I suggest you begin looking for a new job while you are currently in one (and have enough energy for the search). If a bad work situation is not likely to change in the near future, you should protect yourself—your physical, mental, and emotional health.

Change Bad Habits and Add Good Habits

Anyone who has ever made a New Year's resolution knows that, although well intentioned on January 1, the motivation for changing a bad habit or adding a good habit dissolves by mid-February. We are human, creatures of habit, and not likely to change. Change for us needs to be more purposeful, behavioral, and connected to a greater lifestyle goal, such as your fulfilling career acts.

Think through the changes you would like to make for the sake of improving your career acts in Exercise 13. Think of the bad habits you would like to shed and the good habits you would like to add. Be specific. Make them behavioral. Start small. For example, rather than writing "I'd like to volunteer," write something specific, such as "once a week I will volunteer to walk the dogs at the animal shelter for one hour." Or, instead of writing "I'd like to eat better," write something you can follow, such as "I will have a piece of fruit for my midday snack." Instead of writing "I will protect my time," write something fairly straightforward, such as "I will keep the TV off one day per week." The small and manageable changes are steps toward a greater goal, improved physical and emotional health. Use Exercise 13 to write some specific behaviors to achieve a healthier you.

As we've seen in this chapter, managing multiple career acts requires increased mental acuity, physical stamina, and emotional strength. Above all, take proper care of yourself and recharge your life's batteries before taking on an additional career act.

Exercise 13: Changing Habits to Improve Your Mental, Physical, and Emotional Well-Being

Improve Mental, Physical, and Emotional Well-Being

Name three bad habits you would like to kick to have better mental, physical, and emotional well-being:

1. _____

2. _____

3. _____

Name three good habits you would like to start to have better mental, physical, and emotional well-being:

1. _____

2. _____

3. _____

chapter six

Protect and Leverage Your Time, Money, and Human Resources

"We never know the worth of water 'til the well is dry."
English Proverb

The person in control of your career is *you*. You control where you want to spend your talent, your time, and your energy. You control which career act will receive the most attention and when that attention will be given.

You are in control.

Too many Americans are feeling out of control today. A 2008 study conducted by the American Psychological Association (APA) found that one third of Americans state that they live with *extreme stress*, and almost half claim that the stress they experience is having a negative effect on everything from their health, their relationships, and their work. Approximately 75% of Americans report that *money* and *work* are the sources of their stress. This number is unfortunately up over 15% from the previous year.

Having control over your two main stressors, money and work, are within your control if you actively and strategically direct your career to have the wealth-creating career acts that you enjoy. I have said in numerous places in this book that I do not advocate you working longer hours, nor do I want you to worsen your work-life balance by trying to do multiple time-consuming jobs for the sake of money.

I advocate finding multiple interesting income-creating activities, career acts of the things you most enjoy doing, for the sake of freedom. Direct attention to the acts you believe deserve the highest priority.

To learn how to avoid work-related stress, you first need to understand how it forms. Most researchers who study job stress define it as *"the harmful physical and emotional responses that occur when the requirements of the job do not match the capabilities, resources, or needs of the worker" (NIOSH, 1999).*[1] Burnout, an extreme form of work-related stress, is the result of prolonged exposure to a stressful work environment where an employee lacks control over changing or complex work situations and is unable to perceive benefits despite contributing increased effort. Ongoing exposure to stressful working conditions is hazardous to your physical and mental well-being. Anyone who ever feels exhausted after a stressful day of work knows that this is true.

Workplace stress is the relationship between the work-related demands on the employee and the amount of control or support that he or she has to meet the demands.[2] *High demands, low control,* and *low support* combine to produce work-related stress. Many misperceptions people have about work-related stress stem from a lack of understanding of how these three elements work together. From discussions I have had as a career coach, the three most common misperceptions about job stress are as follows:

- **Misperception 1: Those who are the most successful in their careers are also the most stressed; you cannot have it all**—Although it is true that added responsibilities can be a source of stress, it is also true that those with higher-level and better-paid roles tend to have *greater resources* to be effective in those roles and *more control* over how they accomplish their tasks. These resources and control translate into lower stress levels, not higher ones.

- **Misperception 2: Managing people causes stress**—Yes, people are unpredictable. They have a myriad of dispositional and personal problems that can make managing them a challenge. However, if you select your team well, the people who work for you can lower your work-related stress tremendously. Having motivated and talented people working for you is an excellent way to *increase your resources.* Many managers also have the ability to delegate tasks, giving them *greater control* over their own work.

- **Misperception 3: Working part-time (or in a low-paying routine job) will reduce work-related stress because there will be no pressure to perform**—Similar to the first misperception, it is generally the case that the lower you are in the organizational chart, the less control you have over how you perform your tasks and how you allocate your time and resources. Unfortunately, those who believe that part-time or more routine work will lower their stress level usually find the opposite to be true. They are under the greatest pressure because they have the *least control* over the work they do and the *fewest available resources.*

As all of these misperceptions suggest, when control and resources increase, work-related stress levels decline—even in the face of greater responsibilities and demands. In the current economic climate, with the many layoffs and cost-cutting measures, companies

---

Get a Life, Not a Job Advice

✓ Don't trust people who continually tell you that you "cannot have it all." People who hold you back mentally from attaining your goals do not have your best interests in mind.

✓ Protect your resources—your time, money, and human resources.

✓ Try to add a source of passive income to your career.

✓ Invest in your career acts. You'll need to spend money to make money.

are asking their employees to do more with fewer resources. Even those with stable full-time jobs (and successful entrepreneurs) are feeling work-related stress as resources are squeezed from every level.

I am encouraging you to add career acts, which, by definition, means that you will likely be increasing your responsibilities. Some of this career act stress might be *eustress,* or "good stress"—the type of stress that is associated with excitement, joy, and pride in your accomplishments. And some career-related stress has the potential to be traditional stress (the bad kind). If a new career act increases your responsibility demand-side, without a corresponding increase in the supply of available resources, your stress level is bound to increase also.

To keep your stress level low (or limited to good stress), we need to discuss the supply-side of this equation: your ability to increase your available resources (time, money, people) and control over the work you do. *The last thing I want to do is create more stress in your life.*

In Chapter 5, "Increase Your Mental, Physical, and Emotional Well-Being," I encourage you to increase your energy level by improving your health. If you improve your health—your overall mental, physical, and psychological wellness—your available resources will increase immediately because you will have more energy. Energy is a resource—one that enables you to move faster, think more clearly, and act more purposefully. By increasing the supply of this previous resource, you should be able to benefit from a lower overall stress level.

In addition to increasing your physical, emotional, and mental well-being, *what other resources can you marshal to add additional career acts* without *adding stress?* There are three: *time, money (financial resources),* and *people (human resources).*

I cannot offer more hours in a day. With respect to money, I wish I could snap my fingers, wiggle my nose, and immediately add zeros to your bank statement. As we all know, it is not that easy. Likewise, it would be nice if I could send you a well-qualified, highly organized personal assistant. I cannot. Although there is no magic to offer, there are realistic ways to stretch and grow your time, financial resources, and human resources to better control and grow your career acts. Let's talk about all three.

Time and Your Career Acts

Americans consider time to be a commodity. We spend time. We waste time. We buy time. We make time. As much as we believe we can control the commodity of time, there are still only 24 hours in a day. What you do with those 24 hours each day will greatly influence the success of your career.

Countless books and articles have been written about time management. Over the years, passively or actively, we have been taught numerous time-saving techniques: how to answer e-mails expeditiously, how to politely cut off long-winded colleagues when they are taking up too much of our time, how to preplan and cook meals so we can save time on dinner preparation, and how to organize our closets to save minutes otherwise wasted on wardrobe indecision every morning. *When did we become so desperate to reclaim time that we need patronizing advice on writing, talking, eating, and dressing ourselves?* Please.

You don't need time-management advice. You need to rethink your relationship with time. You need to fall in love with the 24 hours you have each day. Love your time. Respect your time. Protect your time. (I feel like am writing a marital vow.) You need to care so deeply about your time that the way you use it is carefully guarded.

With the inception of more sophisticated technologies, we seem to include more activities into the same 24 hours than we had before—text messaging, social media networking (Facebook, YouTube, Twitter), 24-hour news Web sites, and the list goes on. While we pour more activities into each day to feed our insatiable activity appetites, we are becoming perpetually time famished. We need to control our appetites for activity and began respecting and protecting our time.

Parents tell their children to not talk to strangers, not to walk alone, and not to stay out past dark. These rules are made to protect children because children are vulnerable. Think of protecting the hours in your day with the same sense of diligence. Like your children, your hours are also vulnerable to many nefarious elements. *How many can you name?* I'll start: mindless TV viewing, pointless Internet surfing, recreational shopping, and curiosity-driven time on social-networking sites. The underlying theme of these activities is that they are all meaningless. They lack purpose and they deprive us of the precious time we need to grow our amazing, income-generating career acts. They steal from our vulnerable hours and give us nothing in return.

What you want to include in that day and how you spend your time is entirely your decision and should be completely determined by the rules you create to protect your time. These rules should be guided by what is most fulfilling to you in your personal life, social life, family life, and work life. Exercise 14 should shed some light on how well you have been respecting and protecting your time.

Turn Off Your TV (and Everything Else Both Wired and Wireless)

According to the A.C. Nielsen Company, the average American watches more than four hours of TV each day.[3] Doing nothing else except turning off your television set, you can reclaim enough time for

Exercise 14: Your Activity Log

For one week, at the end of each day, write down the two most fulfilling activities of the day and the two most meaningless activities of the day. Estimate the amount of time spent on each. What pattern do you see?

Monday

The two most fulfilling activities of today were _____
and _____.

The time spent on fulfilling activity 1: _____.

The time spent on fulfilling activity 2: _____.

The two most meaningless activities of today were _____
and _____.

The time spent on meaningless activity 1: _____.

The time spent on meaningless activity 2: _____.

Tuesday

The two most fulfilling activities of today were _____
and _____.

The time spent on fulfilling activity 1: _____.

The time spent on fulfilling activity 2: _____.

The two most meaningless activities of today were _____
and _____.

The time spent on meaningless activity 1: _____.

The time spent on meaningless activity 2: _____.

Wednesday

The two most fulfilling activities of today were _____
and _____.

The time spent on fulfilling activity 1: _____.

The time spent on fulfilling activity 2: _____.

The two most meaningless activities of today were _____
and _____.

The time spent on meaningless activity 1: _____.

The time spent on meaningless activity 2: _____.

and so on. . .

Generally, Exercise 14 sheds some light on how well you have been respecting and protecting your time. If there is room for improvement, the following sections discuss a few suggestions for respecting and protecting your time.

---

an outstanding career act. *Thinking back over your last month of TV viewing, what shows do you really remember? Which ones are so entertaining that they are worth watching recreationally?*

If you watch or surf or text or do anything blindly, you are not respecting and protecting your vulnerable and valuable time. However, you might have a TV program, video game, or online poker tournament that you view as a meaningful use of time because it is a source of recreation or relaxation. Ascribing meaning to your activities—whether fulfilling or meaningless—is your decision. *Who am I to tell you what these activities mean to you?* The point is that you are in control of your day, so it is up to you to make sure you use your 24 hours purposefully. Do not blindly turn on your television or computer each evening because you have nothing better to do. You have something much better to do with that precious time: Go out and start a new and interesting career act.

Shed Hassles and Low-Priority Tasks

Another way to respect and protect your time is to reduce the hassles and low-importance tasks. Small changes to the way you manage your errands, such as having your dry cleaning, groceries, and prescriptions delivered, hiring a cleaning person, or setting up your bills to be paid automatically, can save you a great amount of time. Think of the various things in your life that you could automate or outsource.

Leverage Flexible Working Opportunities

If you work for a company, that company might offer various flexible work arrangements that might assist you in juggling your multiple career acts and protecting your time. Flextime and telecommuting, for example, enable you to have greater control and more freedom to allocate your time as you see fit. If you seek a multiple-act career, you might want to consider working for an organization that allows some useful forms of flexible work arrangement.

Likewise, if you seek a multiple-act career, you might want to consider working for an organization offering "family friendly" work-life practices, such as an onsite day care center. These offerings are designed to increase employees' satisfaction, improve retention, and improve employee performance. These practices have the added benefit of helping you manage your responsibilities while enjoying more time for the things you most want to do (for example, spend time with your children, practice a hobby, add a starter job for a new career act).

Concentrate and Focus

Time-management advice tells us that multitasking is an efficient way to squeeze more minutes out of the day. Attempting to apply time-management advice (and not wanting to color-code my closet), I tried multitasking, using my BlackBerry for calls and e-mails while exercising on the treadmill and watching the news on TV. If you listen closely to this book, you will hear the collective groan from my colleagues and research assistants.

There is plenty of science to support why you should not multitask. In study after study,[4] researchers have found that instead of making people more efficient and more productive, multitasking actually wastes time and lowers the quality of what is accomplished. The reason is that the brain's executive function—your "internal CEO"—is designed to concentrate on one task at a time. When you fragment your CEO by trying to do several things at once, you force it to reorient to each task each time you shift back to it from whatever else you're doing.

Try this for five minutes: Watch a TV news program that offers both a story on the screen and a series of headlines scrolling at the bottom. *Can you follow both simultaneously?* Most of us believe we can, but, in truth, we cannot. *If you had to take a quiz on what you just saw, heard, and read, how well would you do?* The participants in numerous studies in cognitive psychology on dichotic listening (listening to multiple things simultaneously) and selective attention (attending and effectively understanding multiple things simultaneously) did not do very well. The fact is that, like it or not, the human brain is limited in how much it can process effectively at one time. Multitasking is, in effect, "exceeding the design specs" of the human brain.

It is very typical to see laptops open in today's college classroom—and taking notes on the computer versus doing it with pen and paper is probably just fine. But students who use laptops often believe they are more efficient when they multitask because they can look up information while the lecture is being presented. In a study conducted by Drs. Hembrooke and Gay, the opposite was found. In an experimental study, students who were allowed to use their laptops to multitask during class scored lower on both recall and recognition tests, compared with those who were not allowed to keep their laptops open. The result held regardless of whether their multitasking browsing was class related.[5]

Even if the tasks are not simultaneous, we also lose time when we keep many tasks going at a single time, changing rapidly from task to task. Drs. Rubinstein, Meyer, and Evans found that individuals in their studies lost time when they changed tasks, and the negative effect of time loss was the greatest when trying to change across multiple complex tasks.[6] It is more efficient to focus on one thing at a time. If you opt to spend your precious time on a meaningful activity in your personal or professional life, concentrate on it. Focus.

We are talking about *effectively* managing more than one career act at a time—not starting many things and scrambling to do them. The latter is what multitasking ends up being.

Let's consider the career acts of Jim and Daniel and analyze how they marshal their resources to grow their career acts.

Jim's career acts—By occupation, Jim is a dentist. After several years of enjoying his occupation and building a successful practice, he decided to add a second act to his career. Jim has a love for wines and an interest in living, at least part-time, in the country. Each summer, he and his wife would vacation in wine-producing areas of the world, where he found himself drawn to the vineyards, spending time among the grapes and talking to the farmers and the winery owners. He took many wine-making classes and developed an insatiable appetite for learning what it takes to run a winery successfully. He volunteered his time at vineyards during a couple of harvest seasons and, after about seven years of investing time in research, education, and experience, he was ready to add a career act: Jim bought a small winery. He retained the knowledgeable employees who had worked in the winery and hired a manager to oversee the business affairs. Being careful to not allow this second career act to interfere with his first, he arranged his patient schedule and began working with trusted colleagues so he could comfortably be on leave during the harvest months of September and October, as well as taking several long weekends during the year. The integration of the two career acts has been relatively seamless because Jim had a plan such that neither interfered with the other.

Daniel's career acts—A football player in high school and college, Daniel always enjoyed sports and athletics in general. Daniel also loves music, R&B specifically. As a natural extrovert, Daniel has a need for affiliation and wanted a career that would enable him to interact with people. His career anchor in college drew him toward opportunities to lead others. Because of his interest in athletics, he prepared for working at a health club by studying for a certificate to become a personal trainer. Once he began working as a trainer, Daniel earned the respect of management and was soon offered the job of manager of the personal training division for the club, which was one in a large national chain of health clubs. But Daniel initially refused the promotion because he was also working on the other career act he loves—his R&B band—and it was starting to take off. He knew he would not have the extra time he needed for his second career act if he accepted the managerial role. The demand for his R&B music grew and he became more secure in the schedule of performances on the weekends. The demo tapes were made and the gigs were secure. Daniel now had his Saturday nights occupied with an income-generating activity he loved. He was ready to accept the manager's role and the health club was happy to have him in the role. To satisfy his needs for affiliation, Daniel develops solid professional relationships with the clients of the health club and as a musician. He loves what he does, has the respect of those who work for him, and is currently one of the most successful managers in the health club's chain.

While having different career acts, Jim and Daniel are busy people but their friends and family would describe them as having work-life balance, financial success, and an enviable love for what they do. They both have multiple-act careers and they both manage the various acts of their careers in purposeful ways. They both share three elements of well-managed multiple-act careers:

- **Coordinated career acts**—Both Jim and Daniel opted for career acts that they could coordinate from the perspective of time, money, and location. Career acts should not burden any of your resources; instead, they should work collaboratively. For example, the money from one career act might enable you to begin another career act more comfortably. The days off or free time not occupied by one career act should afford you the time for another career act. Career acts, when well coordinated, will not detract from each other. If you are stressed because of your career acts, you might need to scale back or omit an act.

- **A time schedule**—Jim and Daniel are able to keep their career acts in motion because they have clear times for when they are working on each career act. For Jim it is seasonal. He spends the late summer and early fall at the winery, setting up what is needed for the year. His pattern is followed annually. In my own case, as a professor, I too have an annual pattern, as I try to write as much as I can during the summers when classes are not in session. Daniel has a weekly pattern, working at the gym during the week and his music on the weekends. Jim, in addition to his annual pattern, also has a daily pattern. He checks for wine orders on the Web site every morning before going to his first act, his dental office. He works on billing and marketing ideas for the winery for a few hours each weekend. The pattern works well for him and has evolved over the years.

- **Career acts that grow purposefully**—In your career, be careful not to take more than what you can manage effectively and successfully. This is particularly important if you have never managed multiple concurrent important roles. Start your multiple-act career slowly. Build it methodically. Keep it manageable, comfortable, and stress free for you.

Freeing Even More Time: Create Sources for Passive Income

If your overarching ideal career act is to spend *no time* (or very little time) engaged in income-creating activities, you should consider ways to build your sources of passive income (money that is paid to you for a product or service that does not require your active involvement or time). The three most typical sources of passive income are royalties, affiliate marketing, and rent.

Let's consider royalties first. As a source of passive income, royalties are based on your creation of and ownership of (for example, copyright or patent) something, such as a book, product, or service that you turn over to someone or some other company to sell. The creation of passive income happens when you omit yourself from the next steps, the sales and marketing of whatever you created. (Finding a buyer, a publisher, or a marketing firm is not a small step.) Whenever they sell your product or book or use your approach, you receive a royalty. Checks are sent (direct deposited, even better) without much additional time on your part, beyond your initial investment.

Affiliate marketing is an Internet-based approach you could consider if you have an active Web site. Vendors will pay you (the affiliate) a commission each time someone clicks on their product or purchases their product from your site.

Another source of passive income is rent from property you own. Owning and renting property is a common career act. For the property to be a true source of *passive* income (i.e., no additional investment of time), you need to hire a real estate management company to maintain your property and manage tenant relations. Only when others are taking care of these daily challenges (and there can be many) does rent become a true source of passive income. You will be paying for the service of the management company, but your time is free for you to spend however you want.

Royalties, affiliate marketing, and rents are three suggestions for passive income if you value your time and want to create sources of passive income. Finding and building sources of passive income take some initial investment of time, energy, and (usually) money—but when they are successful, they are wonderfully liberating.

I can illustrate sources of passive income created through one of my career acts. In 1995, after completing my Ph.D. and before starting with Rutgers, I developed some international career-related tools that are now used by companies all over the world. In truth, they are outstanding tools, but in the late 1990s (and probably today), I was really lousy at selling them. In 2001, I conceded that I lacked any natural gift for sales, and I handed the tools to Mike Schell for his company in the same field, RW-3, to sell. This risky move was made easier by the fact that I've known Mike for years and trusted him to do the right thing. Mike, liking the tools and knowing me very well, knew he could make more money for me than I could on my own. In getting out of my own way, I now generate revenue passively through the sale of these tools. My investment and risk paid off.

Let's return to the concept of multiple sources of income for a moment with respect to creating sources of passive income. This strategy (and the reason it was not difficult to hand over the tools for someone else to sell) was made easier by the fact that I was a professor at Rutgers and engaged in HR consulting. These two other career acts were already in motion, making the leap for passive income fairly low risk. It would have been much more difficult to hand over the tools if the revenue from their sales was my only source of income. If you would like to build your sources of passive income, I would suggest you use the ideas of a multiple-act career to build them with less financial risk.

Financial Resources and Your Career Acts

There are only three ways to raise additional money to fund the start or growth of a career act: You can *save money.* You can *earn money.* You can *borrow money. How much money do you need to start an additional career act?* The answer, of course, depends on the nature of the career act and whether getting it started will require an investment in education, materials, equipment, and the like. To become a physician, from the beginning of the undergraduate premed program through completion of medical school, might cost between $100,000 and $300,000 in the educational investment alone. At the other end of the scale, selling your watercolor paintings at a local art festival might cost only $10 to $30 to rent booth space for the weekend. The financial return on each of these investments is likely to be proportional to the investment: The weekend artist will likely make less than the physician. The emotional returns, however, might be equivalent.

What career act do you really want and what financial resources will you need to invest to achieve them? With respect to investment in career acts, there is some truth in the cliché: *You need to spend money to make money.*

Please don't let the price tag of a career act hold you back from pursuing it. Instead, be realistic about what the costs might be and whether you can afford those costs without increasing your stress to an uncomfortable level. Think through Exercise 15 to try to estimate the costs to start and grow in your ideal career acts.

Exercise 15: Funding Your Career Acts

The following are some ways to gain knowledge about the financial resources required to begin your career acts:

1. Talk to several people who are currently in your ideal career act.

    a. Ask them to describe the investments they made along the way in terms of education, training, equipment, certificates, licensures, office space, systems, and the like.

    b. Ask each person, "What do you believe was the best investment you made in your career?"

    c. Be sure to ask more than one person, so that you can see if there are consistent themes among people who are successful in the career act you are contemplating.

2. Generate a comprehensive and realistic funding list.

    a. Read about your ideal career act from reputable Web sites and publications, such as professional or trade associations. Estimate the cost, if any, for your preparation (e.g., education and training) or anything else your interviewees might not have mentioned (for example, developing a Web site). Understand that requirements for your career act might have changed since your interviewees were first beginning their careers, so you might need *to add some items to your initial funding list.*

142

    b. If your starter career act is an entrepreneurial venture, such as opening a catering business, a day spa, or the next hot social networking site, please visit the Small Business Association's Web site at www. sba.gov. Another useful source is your local Small Business Development Center (SBDC), which you can locate by a ZIP Code search on www.asbdc-us.org/. If you are female, look into the National Association of Women Business Owners (www.nawbo.org/); and if you are a minority group member, the Minority Owned Business Development Agency (www.mbda.gov/) might be helpful. These organizations offer many tools to help you determine the financial needs for your new enterprise. Are there other financial resources you will need to start your business and keep it afloat while you build your business (e.g., marketing, inventory, insurance)? *Add these items to your funding list.*

3. Compile the total amount of money you will need.

    a. Review your funding list and research what those investments would cost in today's dollars. What is your funding total?

    b. Add 20% to the total. This is your new required *funding total* for your career act. (Remember, I am hoping to keep your stress level down; I have never heard anyone complain that they saved too much money.)

From Exercise 15, you can make a rough estimate of what the total cost associated with your career act might be. If your ideal career act is to be an attorney or physician, your list might have more zeros than if your ideal career act is to be a writer or a photographer. Whatever the total funding amount required, *you should have a realistic plan for ways to raise the money needed.* You have three options:

1. Save money.

2. Earn money.

3. Borrow money.

To help you decide what plan you should make for building financial resources to start and grow your career, *try to answer the following questions:*

■ ***How much do you need to start this career act?***—
Review your funding total from Exercise 15 (question 3b).

- *How much have you already saved for starting this career act? Is it enough to start your career act?*—If you are starting an entrepreneurial venture, please keep in mind that the Small Business Administration[7] reports that about two thirds of new businesses will survive their first two years, but only 44% will last for four years. In large part, this high rate of failure is because the small businesses are often underfunded from the onset and underestimate ongoing expenses. Please consider all of the possible expenses, both start-up and ongoing, before diving into the venture.

- *Can one career act help finance another (even temporarily)?*—This might be the case if you are working during the day and going to school in the evening or if you are developing an entrepreneurial venture on the weekends and working during the week.

- *Is your spouse or partner able to support the funding of this career act, as an investment in your family?*—In many cases, a spouse or partner works full-time and earns enough to support the couple while the other spouse or partner starts a new career act. Sometimes couples will take turns working at full-time jobs until they both attain the career acts they enjoy. Couples might also agree to scale back their collective expenses temporarily while building their career acts.

- *How much income can you realistically anticipate generating from this career act, and how soon?*—This is especially true for career acts requiring a major investment, such as years of education and training, or a large lump-sum initial expense in starting a new business. For example, since the late 1990s, there has been a shortage of nurses, and this is expected to continue past 2025 as the population ages and requires more medical care. If you complete nursing school, you can be almost guaranteed a financially rewarding full-time job as soon as you pass the licensure examination to become an RN. On the other hand, if you return to school for a master's degree in art history with a specialization on Ming dynasty Chinese ceramics, you might need a longer time frame to find an ideal career act.

- *What is your comfort level with debt?*—This is a soul-searching question. Some people are optimistic to the point of almost being reckless with money, whereas others need to be reminded that it's financially wise to spend some money (invest in yourself) to make some money (and enjoy what you are doing).

Whatever the total funding amount required, *you should have a realistic plan for ways to raise the money needed.* The way many people fund their additional career acts is to allow their current income-generating career act to fund their new one until it, too, becomes profitable. Others need to borrow and save to put the money together to invest in their future career satisfaction.

The truth is that great careers almost always require some financial investment. Although being frugal and saving money is sage advice in a risky economy, *no one has ever saved their way to prosperity.* Although Americans are not known for their thrift, it is worth mentioning (especially to those of you who are exceptionally tight with your purse) that you might need to take a well-calculated financial risk and make an investment in yourself. Take a deep breath. Open your wallet. You can do it.

Numerous financial resources are available to you as you invest in your career acts. For investments in education, for example, there are numerous federal loan programs, such as Stafford loans, Perkins loans, Parent PLUS loans, and Graduate PLUS loans. In addition to loans, many colleges and universities offer scholarships (that is, free money) for elite athletes and exceptional scholars. Most colleges and universities also offer need-based and interest-based work-study options (that is, part-time jobs). Some lenders offer career training loans to fund occupational training, such as technical programs, certificate programs, or trade schools. You should conduct a Web search and talk to reputable bank loan officers (for example, from FDIC insured banks) about ways to finance education and training.

If you have an idea for a small business and have written it up in a solid business plan, you might be eligible for a loan from the federal government's Small Business Administration (SBA). The SBA provides a number of financial assistance programs for small businesses, most in the form of loans in conjunction with banks. It also provides information on how to apply for a number of nonprofit grants. Please be aware that business lending is not regulated as carefully as home mortgage lending, and be careful to avoid predatory lenders preying on would-be entrepreneurs. Be suspicious of any organization that offers to lend you money without assessing your business plan—and in general, if an offer of financing sounds too good to be true, it probably is. Do the arithmetic carefully: *How much will you actually be paying by the time the loan is paid off? Are there application fees, loan initiation fees, or prepayment fees? And what are the penalties if your business fails and you default on the loan?*

If you need a larger amount of capital than what an SBA loan will cover, you might need to consider trying to attract venture capitalists or "angel" investors. The trade-off is that angel investors and venture capitalists will generally take a share of your business and look for a relatively fast return on their investment. The SBA loans, while more modest, leave you in complete control. There are numerous books and Web sites available to help you navigate the information related to loans and other ways to raise capital for small businesses.

The opening sentence of a recent article in the *International Herald Tribune* made me smile: "Watching Americans try to make themselves frugal is like watching Mongolians try to make Bordeaux wine."[8] Ouch. The truth hurts, even delivered collectively. I have worked in many countries all throughout this great planet and, it is true, we Americans like our stuff. We have an unbelievable amount of stuff that we do not need. We shop recreationally to buy more stuff. We rent storage units to collect our stuff. Without too much pain and effort, most of us Americans could probably save money simply by deciding, starting right now, to buy less new stuff. You can probably think of other small changes you could make—clipping coupons, car pooling, drinking regular coffee instead of a custom-blended latte—that would leave you with more money in your wallet at the end of each month. In an effort to reclaim some resources, especially your financial resources, try to better understand if you are wasting resources. As you become more aware of the waste in your life, you can change some behaviors to free up resources for your career acts. Let's consider Exercise 16. (This one is probably much easier to do online at www.PaulaCaligiuri.com.)

Exercise 16: Estimating Waste in Your Discretionary Income to Be Used for Your Career Acts

From a financial perspective, investing in your career might be much easier than you think. If you are like many working adults, you probably have some discretionary income. Discretionary income is the amount remaining from your income after you have paid your taxes, insurance, rent/mortgage, and all other life essentials, such as your housing, food, and clothing.

How much discretionary income do you have? Use the Disposable Income Calculator found at www.disposableincome.net to make that estimate. After completing the calculator, fill in the number from the summary statement, "That leaves you _____ per hour for whatever you want." Now multiply the number you just wrote by 8,760. This is the estimate of your discretionary income each year.

Can you reinvest some of your disposable income in yourself—*without* changing your lifestyle? The answer is probably yes. Try the following exercise (you might prefer to do this exercise online at www.PaulaCaligiuri.com):

1. Estimate how many nonreference books you have on your bookshelves. (A) _____. Estimate how many of them you have read or realistically plan on reading in the next year. (B) _____ Calculate the percent of (A) represented by (B): _____ *(1)*

2. Count the number of shirts you have that are less than 3 years old. (A) ____ Count how many of those you have worn in the past year. (B) ____ Calculate the percent of (A) represented by (B): _____ *(2)*

3. Count all of the items in your refrigerator. (A) ____ Count all of the items that are either past their expiration date or, if they are fresh, cannot possibly be consumed before they spoil. (B) ____Calculate the percent of (A) represented by (B): _____ *(3)*

4. Count how many corded, cordless, wired, or wireless things you own. (Select your favorite category—power tools, electronics, or kitchen gadgets.) (A) ____ Count how many of these you have used more than twice since purchasing them. (B) ____ Calculate the percent of (A) represented by (B): _____ *(4)*

Add all four percentages (1) + (2) + (3) + (4) and divide by four.

Based on this rough estimate, without missing anything you currently use, have, or enjoy, how much money can you reclaim by merely protecting it from wasteful spending?

The more important question, how could you reinvest that amount of money back into one of your career acts? The possibilities are endless. Here are some examples:

- Take a class.
- Develop a Web site.
- Attend a trade show.
- Buy equipment.
- Start a blog.
- Buy a computer.
- Purchase software.
- Hire a person to help you with household chores to free up more of your time.
- Attend a seminar.
- Take someone to lunch (that is, a person who might be able to help you with your career act).

If you have taken the time to work through Exercise 16, you are probably shocked with the amount of money you can reclaim and invest in yourself without missing anything or changing any behaviors. Thinking seriously before spending money that could otherwise be used to reinvest in you is sage advice. I do not believe saving money is the only way to attain your career goals.

Before you clip and cut your way through your expenses, think through their long-term implications for your career acts. For example, a hobby might seem like an unnecessary expense—but, before you sell your art supplies or your tuba, consider whether your hobby has the potential to be an income generator in the future. Tuba lessons, anyone? Giving up your $20-per-hour cleaning person might be a way to save money, but the hours you can invest in yourself by having someone else clean your house might be worth the investment. Skipping this year's trade show might save money, but the loss of potential contacts and ideas might be the wrong item to cut from your budget. You can see the pattern. It is about investing in your future career acts. Only you can assess the seriousness of your financial circumstances and determine where and how you can most wisely save the money you need.

Let's consider the career acts of Ted:

Ted's career acts—When Ted was in college, he worked as a residence assistant (RA) to help pay for his studies. His job was to monitor and plan activities for the undergraduate students living in his residence hall. After he completed his bachelor's degree and went on to a master's program in marketing, Ted's experience and talent as an RA led him to become a graduate resident and then an assistant director of residential and judicial affairs. Although this career path was unplanned, Ted found that he enjoyed the student interaction and life as a graduate student. What began as a source of funding for Ted turned into a rewarding career act. When Ted completed his master's degree, he left the halls of academe for the halls of corporate America. Ted has had a series of very successful consulting-oriented positions in large U.S.-based firms. In the most recent round of layoffs with his current firm, Ted survived. Although he was not laid off, his confidence in a single career act was shaken. He decided to begin adding some career acts.

Because he was still employed in a comfortable financial situation, his current position enabled him to grow his other career acts. Ted had been scuba diving since he was 16. He took time to complete his advanced training and became a certified scuba instructor. He began to teach scuba diving part-time. Ted is enjoying both the scuba and the teaching experiences. His longer-term career act goal is to offer dive tours and possibly open a diving school. The experience of offering part-time instruction now is helping him create the type of school he would like to offer down the road. Reconnecting with his love for student interaction, Ted has begun to teach at the community college one night per week and has volunteered to counsel students about their own careers for a nonprofit organization. Career counseling and teaching are becoming additional viable career acts for the future.

In Ted's case, he never needed to borrow money because his first career act funded the subsequent ones. His work with residence life enabled him to complete multiple degrees. His work with his current employer is now enabling him to begin career acts in scuba instruction, counseling, and teaching. Ted's is a best-case scenario because he never needed to overburden his financial resources. Now let's consider two more individuals' careers.

Tom V.'s career acts—Tom is a police officer with 35 years of experience. He currently runs the shooting range for his city's police force; this is Tom's primary career act. About 15 years ago, Tom needed to make some extra money and provide financial freedom for his family, so he began an exterminating business for times when he was off duty. He was self-taught in the "bug business" and, when he started, he learned much of what he knows from talking to more seasoned exterminators. Eradicating problems with pesky bugs and rodents, although more predictable than pesky people breaking the law, is an additional career act.

Tom also has a third career act, which originated from his passion for antique trucks. With the money made from his successful exterminating business, Tom opened a restoration garage where others who share the same hobby can pay (well, mostly barter) to use the tools and lifts available. Although in financial terms the garage is only a relatively small career act, Tom finds it the most enjoyable facet of his work life. Recently, Tom has been able to hire employees to work in his exterminating business, freeing him to dedicate more time and energy to the restoration garage.

Tom V.'s example was well planned and financially sound. Sometimes, we do not have the luxury as far as Tom did in advance.

Now let's consider the career acts of Ralph:

Ralph's career acts—Ralph worked on the assembly line for an appliance manufacturing organization. He enjoyed the camaraderie with his colleagues more than his work, but stayed with the job for the salary and benefits. He longed to own his own business but did not have the impetus or financial resources to become an entrepreneur. This changed about two years ago, when Ralph started hearing rumors that his plant was slated to close in 10 months. He needed to support his wife and two children, and did not want to move out of the neighborhood. He started investigating possible businesses to own. After some due diligence, Ralph decided to buy a paper shredding truck. The truck is driven to places like hospitals and lawyers' offices to shred documents securely in their parking lots. The truck cost $75,000 to purchase used. Using home equity lines of credit, a loan from his in-laws, and his severance money once the plant closed, Ralph bought the truck. Before the plant was closed, Ralph began generating clients, mostly from personal contacts. By the time the plant closed, he had a big enough client base to cover the minimum payments on his loans and hire two part-time hourly workers. Ralph and his wife still needed more money to cover their family's expenses, though. They carefully planned ahead for the estimated eight-month financial shortfall: While Ralph built the business, Ralph's wife took a part-time job in the evenings. They also scaled back their family's spending by not taking a summer vacation and not spending as much at the holidays. In about one year after being laid off, Ralph had almost returned to the level of his salary as an assembly worker. His business is growing even in a difficult economy. He has never been happier than he is now, working for himself, and has plans to expand his business to recycle computer and electronic equipment.

Ralph clearly knew what he was getting himself into and had a realistic idea of how long it would take for his paper-shredding business to turn a profit. Ralph's wife was supportive and returned to work so that Ralph could focus on growing his business.

Once more: There are only three ways to raise additional money to fund a career act: You can *save money*. You can *earn money*. You can *borrow money*. Ted and Tom each did one. Ted saved money while attending school where he worked (which offered free tuition as a benefit). Tom used the earnings from his exterminating business to fund his restoration garage. Ralph and his wife did all three. They cut their discretionary spending to *save money*. Ralph's wife took a part-time job to *earn more money*. The couple also *borrowed money* against their home and from Ralph's in-laws.

Like Ted, Tom, and Ralph, when you make a plan for adding a career act, think through the financial resources you will need to be successful—and be realistic. Many books and Web sites are available to give you tips on all three: *saving, earning,* and *borrowing* money. If your funding total for your career act seems out of reach, I suggest you spend some time investigating the many possibilities for educational and business loans.

Human Resources and Your Career Acts

Up to this point in the chapter, I've talked about time and financial resources. But other very important resources are the resources found in those who work for you. The people who work for you extend your own capacity when you delegate some of your tasks. This can lower your stress level by freeing you to do more demanding and critical (and, hopefully, interesting) tasks. Even if you don't have employees working for you, a variety of human resources are available to you to help you with your tasks and balance your stress equation.

Temporary Task-Based Assistance

The concept of working for multiple task-based clients is becoming much more popular. Today many professionals and "virtual assistants" offer their services as freelancers, by the task or job. For example, a bookkeeper might charge for the accounts he handles, such as the number of invoices sent. A customer service professional might charge you only for the service calls she completes. An editor charges you to edit only the documents you send him. Without adding staff, you can add a bookkeeper, a customer service professional, and an editor to shed some of your tasks. If you are starting a small business, consider these freelance or "per diem" professionals as a possible way to extend your own resources. I personally have had great luck with eLance.com for project assistance.

Commission-Based Assistance

Similar to leveraging the skills of task-based professionals, you can also consider hiring people to sell for you and your business. You pay only for the sales they actually make, giving the sales rep a percentage of your gross as his or her commission.

Bartered Assistance

This is a time-honored approach to extend your own resources by swapping what you do well (and easily) for what another person does well (and easily). For example, you can offer to cook dinners for your next-door neighbor two nights a week in exchange for her doing the bookkeeping for your small business. It is likely that you were cooking dinner twice a week anyhow, and doubling the amount of food to serve two households does not take more of your time.

Direct Reports

If you are currently working for an organization or are an entrepreneur and have people reporting to you, please remember that having the right people (with the necessary skill set) in the right place (working on useful tasks) at the right time is critical for your ability to perform your career act well. The following are some basic rules of managing human resources to maximize the intangible asset of having assistance or direct reports:

- **Select well**—There is no single more important task than employee selection when it comes to managing your direct reports. People will bring with them their knowledge, skills, and abilities, but also their motivation and commitment. Select for the skills most necessary for the job. Select for the other attributes affecting the individual's ability to be effective working on your team. You might want to involve some of the team members (those with whom the person will work) to participate in the selection process. Whether you are a sole proprietor about to add your first employee or work for a large firm hiring a person to work in your business unit, remember that every person has the ability to change the culture or effectiveness of the unit. Take this step seriously. The people you hire will have an immediate and direct effect on your own career acts. They will either decrease your stress level by extending your available resources or—if you choose the wrong individuals—add to your stress in any of a host of ways.

- **Train effectively**—Once your direct reports have been working for you for a short time, you will have a better sense of their strengths and the areas in which they need development. Think of training as an investment in building necessary knowledge, skills, and abilities among your direct reports. Training is essential and should be thought of as a priority investment into the future of your own career act. Again, think about the ways your direct reports extend your ability to be more effective in your career act, whether working for yourself with one employee or for a larger organization.

- **Develop and expand roles in meaningful ways**—It is possible, but unlikely, that the job you offer might be your direct report's ideal career act. Remember that those who work for you are aspiring to stimulating and income-generating activities just as you are. When thinking about your direct reports, you might want to consider how the job you offer fits into the scheme of their individual career acts. Even if you cannot offer what is most fulfilling to them, you might want to talk about how they would like to develop their careers to become more motivating in the future. Understanding what a person's key motivators are will unlock their potential and extend you in wonderful ways.

The best manager I ever had was my former dean and dear friend, Professor Barbara Lee. Barbara unlocked potential in me because she took the time to understand what motivated me and offered roles to align with those motivations and benefit our academic department. For example, after I received tenure, she encouraged me to leverage the two things she knew would be most motivating to me: to work in an entrepreneurial way and to work internationally. As a developmental experience, Barbara encouraged me to start the Center for HR Strategy at Rutgers University. This activity stoked my entrepreneurial fire and was a source of funding for faculty research; it also extended our reach into the practitioner community. Likewise, Barbara allowed me to build an international executive master's program, knowing my love for and interest in international research. I share this story to reinforce the point that supervising others can be a win-win: You can advance yourself and others concurrently. Barbara was able to identify developmental opportunities that would advance the unit she ran—but also advance me and keep me motivated. If you have direct reports, I encourage you to align your direct reports' dominant motivators with the developmental opportunities you offer.

- **Motivate and appreciate**—There are perhaps no two more powerful words for motivating your direct reports than the words "thank you." When you say the words, be sure they are meaningful and sincere, matching the behaviors you would like to see repeated. The common advice to "catch them doing something right"—and express your appreciation on the spot—is extremely wise, and not followed often enough. There is no faster way to douse your employees' fire or energy than to underappreciate them.

  Honestly, I really despise Administrative Professionals Day—and every other "day-on-the-calendar" appreciation day. Yes, I think it is important to do nice things and show appreciation—but appreciate a specific behavior, something you would like the employee to repeat. Unless you are personally great friends with your direct reports, taking them out to lunch is not motivating for them. (No offense intended.) Rather, if you feel the need to offer your employee a lunch, give a gift certificate to a restaurant that can be used with the person of his or her choice.

Work through Exercise 17 as a way to better leverage the talents of your direct reports in a way that will be a win-win—advancing your own career act while you advance theirs.

Exercise 17: Human Resources and Career Act Success

For each of your direct reports or employees, try to answer the following questions:

- First consider whether this is a starter career act, an ideal career act, or unrelated to what the person really wants to be doing in his or her career.

- Now think about how this person extends you from the perspective of enhancing your available resources. Is this person performing in a way that frees up some of your resources? How can this person's role be increased?

Name of Direct Report or Employee
What are some things especially motivating to him or her?
1. _____
2. _____
3. _____
What training needs does he or she have, and how will you fill those needs?
1. _____
2. _____
3. _____
How will you develop this employee based on his or her motivators?
1. _____
2. _____
3. _____

Which behaviors do you most want to motivate, and how will you reward and show appreciation for those behaviors?

1. _____

2. _____

3. _____

As I mentioned at the start of this chapter, there is no magic available to effortlessly and immediately grow the hours in a day, your financial resources, or your human resources. But I hope I have given you some tips for how to protect and effectively leverage all three. Depending on your desired career acts and the point in your work life you are starting from, it might not cost much money or take much time to grow these resources—but it will take some thoughtful consideration and planning.

chapter seven

Get a Life: Integrate Your Career with Your Life Priorities

"Action expresses priorities."
Gandhi

If you won four million dollars in a lottery today, would you still want to have a career? Think about it for a moment.

Drs. Richard Arvey, Itzhak Harpaz, and Hui Liao found that lottery winners (average winning almost $4 million) do not automatically quit working. They found that about 85% of them continue working in some form. The level of centrality and importance work plays in the lottery winners' lives factored into their decision regarding whether to continue working. These researchers note that *"although individuals may have continued to work, they also may have modified the type and conditions of their work experiences (e.g., by starting another business or by dropping to part-time work)."*[1] In other words, they worked in ways that were consistent with their work-related values and the goals they had for their careers.

If you are reading this, it means that you have read a book on improving your career (and your life) almost to the end. On this piece of evidence alone, chances are high that you care about how you spend your time in income-generating activities. Like the high-dollar lottery winners who continued working, you want to focus on the stimulation that can be gained from doing the things you enjoy most. Also like the high-dollar lottery winners, you want a stimulating career but you want it on your terms, consistent with your career-related values—and leaving enough time and emotional resources for those you love. The big news: You do not need to win the lottery to make this happen.

This chapter covers the two factors that most directly affect your ability to manage the multiple spheres of your life: your career-related values and your mindfulness across all spheres of your life.

Your Values and Your Career Acts

Above and beyond the type of career acts you would enjoy and find stimulating, there are three career-related values that set the comfort level or boundaries for life. Values, in general, form the foundation for an individual's belief of what is good or bad, right or wrong, positive or negative. As you carry out your career acts, your values will manifest in many ways, such as how many hours per day you will work, how much you are willing to work from home, whether you make friends with colleagues from work, and the level of difficulty of the goals you set for yourself.

Let's consider the three most relevant career-related values affecting the boundaries you will set for your career:

- **Career centrality**—How central is your career as a part of your identity? To what extent does *what you do* define *who you are?* If you are a lottery winner with high career centrality, you will still want to work because to stop working would limit or change your identity in an uncomfortable or undesirable way. On the other hand, if you are lower in career centrality, you will not define yourself as strongly by your career. As a result, you will be able to change in and out of work and nonwork roles more readily.

- **Achievement orientation**—Your achievement orientation or personal drive to succeed is also an important career-related value. This manifests in how hard you are willing to push to succeed, how many risks you are willing to take to achieve your career goals, and how high the goals are that you set for yourself. If you are a strongly achievement-oriented lottery winner, you will likely continue working toward "stretch" career goals even though you don't need the money. You would enjoy your career for the stimulation it provides.

- **Comfort with work-life overlap**—The comfort level you have allowing the spheres of your life to comingle influences your preferences for harmonizing your career with your family life and social life. *Are you someone who places a high value on keeping your personal affairs to yourself when you are at work?* To the extent that you socialize with your business colleagues, *do you see them separately from your personal friends and family?* Or, at the other end of the scale, *do you make a point of sharing the significant events and people in your personal life with your business colleagues?* As a lottery winner, someone who has an affinity for high work-life overlap might enjoy nothing better than using the winnings to start a new business, a nonprofit organization, etc.

There are not correct levels of work centrality, achievement orientation, and comfort with work-life overlap. Each of these values is unique to you, and together they shape the decisions you make about your career. The more aware you are of how you hold these values, the better you can make career decisions that you will be satisfied with over the long term. These values provide the boundaries for maintaining your work-life balance. Consider the questions in Exercise 18 to better understand your career-related values.

Exercise 18: Your Career-Related Values

Instructions: Following is a quick assessment of your career-related values. Answer the following questions, giving yourself 1 point for each "yes." You can have a maximum of 3 points for each set of questions.

Career Centrality

1. When you fill in the blank, "I am _____," do you think about your professional role first (compared with other roles, such as father, wife, etc.)? ☐ **Yes** ☐ **No**

2. Is success in your career important to you? ☐ **Yes** ☐ **No**

3. Would you still want a career if you did not need to work? ☐ **Yes** ☐ **No**

Achievement Orientation

1. Do you set many career-related goals for yourself? ☐ **Yes** ☐ **No**

2. Do you feel most satisfied with your career when you know you are working toward advancing it? ☐ **Yes** ☐ **No**

3. Do you become frustrated at times when you feel stalled in your career?
☐ **Yes** ☐ **No**

Work-Life Overlap

1. Is it comfortable for you to think about your career when you are not (technically) working (e.g., bringing work home)? ☐ **Yes** ☐ **No**

2. Are you comfortable when your work life and your personal or social life intermix?
☐ **Yes** ☐ **No**

3. Do you have close friends at work who know about your personal life?
☐ **Yes** ☐ **No**

Where you place the three-dimensional boundary between your career and your personal life reflects your work-related values.

- If you score either 2 or 3 on career centrality, you probably place high importance on your career as a facet of your identity. You should, therefore, consider career acts as carefully as you would other major decisions, such as choosing a college or a marriage partner. Your work-related boundaries will expand provided that your career acts are a positive reflection on you.

- If you score either 2 or 3 on achievement orientation, you tend to value the ongoing goal-directed challenges embedded in your career acts. Select career acts where you can continually move ahead and have greater accomplishments. Your work-related boundaries will expand provided your career acts are recognizing your achievements.

- If you score 2 or 3 on work-life overlap, you probably are more comfortable allowing the lines between your work life and your personal life to blur. Your work-related boundaries will expand as your personal life becomes richer and more satisfying; you might enjoy a "virtuous cycle" in which your career and personal life mutually benefit each other.

The better you come to understand your own career-related values, the more self-awareness you will be able to use to navigate career-related decisions. This understanding will also help you to avoid the potential conflicts you might experience between the work and nonwork spheres of your life as you find the appropriate boundaries between the two.

If you are a new graduate at the start of your career, you might need some time and experience before you are able to say what your career-related values are. If you are further in your career, you might see your values beginning to change. Values can form and change over time as the circumstances of our lives change. *Are you able to articulate your career-related values well enough to make decisions consistent with those values?*

Your Career Acts and Your Significant Other

It is important to understand your career-related values and how they influence your relationships with those you love as you engage in your career acts. *Have you heard anyone praising a loved one using any of the following sentiments?*

- "I am so proud of NAME. He/she just received a big promotion at work."
- "NAME's business is doing well. He/she has worked so hard to build that business to what it is today."
- "I am so glad NAME left his/her company. That job was killing him/her. The money is not worth the sacrifice."
- "I give NAME so much credit for going back to school. It will be difficult for us as a family for a while but he/she will finally be able to train to do what he/she loves."
- "I am so proud of NAME. He/she is helping to keep the public safe every day in his/her work as a police officer."

These are all positive sentiments expressed by those who admire and respect the career-related values of their loved ones.

Couples need not share every value—but they do need to have a healthy respect for each other's values. With respect to work-life overlap, there is a level of tolerance that would be needed if the couple's values are different. To illustrate the importance of respecting and tolerating each other's values, think about statements people might make when they are frustrated with their loved ones over career-related issues. *Have you heard any of the following?*

- "NAME is not very motivated. He/she just doesn't care about getting ahead in his/her career and always seems to settle for less."

- "NAME is a workaholic. All he/she cares about is his/her career."
- "NAME cannot leave work where it belongs—at work. He/she continually brings work home."
- "NAME doesn't understand that I am working hard for our future. He/she is not very supportive."
- "NAME lets people at work walk all over him/her. Dedication is one thing, but he/she puts in too much time and energy for too little pay and recognition."

These are all negative sentiments reflected in those who do not respect the career-related values of their loved ones. Chances are very high that you have heard comments like these before.

Let me provide an illustration of how this plays out with one couple, Helen and Tim. Helen and Tim are fictitious characters who have been fused from the very real stories of dozens of men and women I have met over the years. I could change the roles, change the names, and change the jobs, but the story's trajectory would remain the same.

Helen and Tim met and fell in love when they were college students. They were introduced through mutual friends, and quickly found that they had many interests and values in common. They were a loving and respectful couple, communicating well with each other. After graduation, Tim (with his management degree) started working as an assistant manager for a branch of a car rental company. Helen (with her engineering degree) began an entry-level job working in research and development for a medical devices company. Two years after graduation, they were married. As newlyweds, Tim and Helen were not only in love but also very happy with their starter career acts and their new life together.

Prior to their engagement, Tim and Helen had serious conversations about their financial values (both are fiscally conservative), family values (both wanted children), and religious values (they share their faith and attend church together). But unfortunately, they were so new to their careers that their career-related values were still forming. They never discussed their work-related values because they did not know what they were—or even that there was such a thing.

By the time they had been married for a year, it became clear that Tim had a lower career centrality and achievement orientation than Helen; he also had a low tolerance for work-life overlap. He worked hard and was promoted, but Helen felt he lacked a zest for work and did not devote enough energy to planning his future career moves. In Helen's eyes, Tim liked having a job that paid well but it was "just a job." In contrast, as Helen became more involved in her career, she became more and more identified with her job. She had no problem bringing work home with her. In fact, Helen loved the discovery process of her job—the greater the challenge, the more she enjoyed the work. She frequently described how she could not "turn off her brain when she went home" when she was trying to work through an engineering challenge. And this was an annoyance to Tim, who wanted Helen to join him in relaxing and enjoying their leisure time when they were not at work.

Without identifying and respecting the differences in work-related values, Tim and Helen could not understand each other's positions and began to resent each other. Helen thought Tim was "settling" and did not care about his career. Tim thought Helen did not have her priorities right and was giving too much of herself to her job. Both complained that the other partner had "changed" and was not the same person he/she married. After just three years of marriage, they filed for a divorce, citing irreconcilable differences.

Young couples who marry in their early 20s (ages 20 through 24) have a divorce risk of almost 40%—a statistic that drops significantly as marital age increases.[2] The American Academy of Matrimonial Lawyers lists "dramatic change in priorities" as one of the top reasons couples of all ages cite for divorcing.[3] Helen and Tim, unfortunately, illustrate both of these statistics.

Whether as a symptom or a reason for the breakup, the ability to communicate about work-related values would save much heartache. It is important that you are communicating regarding your career-related values. This does not mean that you have to share every value. It does not even mean that you have to know what your values are. What it does mean is that you find a way to work out the boundaries in a way that will be comfortable for both of you.

Setting these boundaries begins with a conversation, an open discussion about how you and your partner will navigate potential differences, rooted in love and respect for the other. Your values will likely change over time, and so will those of your partner. On some values, you might be evenly matched, whereas on others, you might be at opposite extremes. Matching is not necessarily better than being opposites; many couples find that their different work-related values complement each other and make their relationship even richer and more satisfying.

Whatever your work-related values are and however they evolve, remember that for a great career, you need to communicate with those you love, for your nearest and dearest are not in the audience of your career acts—they are an integral part of your career acts. Having a respectful understanding of career values and working through how they affect the other spheres of your life will help enhance your overall life satisfaction tremendously.

Be Mindful in All Spheres of Your Life

In addition to understanding your career-related values, there is another factor that will help you manage your career in conjunction with the other spheres of your life. This is your ability to be fully present or "in the moment" wherever you are, whether at work, at home, playing sports, or caring for your children. This quality of being fully present is something Buddhists call "mindfulness;" it is the opposite of "going through the motions" or "acting on autopilot."

Your career, even your fabulous multiple-act career, is only one sphere of your life. For many people, their family life, their social life, and their private or personal life (including the activities such as hobbies, sports, recreational activities, and participation in a faith community) are the three most important spheres along with their careers. Understanding your career values and practicing mindfulness in all the activities of your life helps to bring those you love with you as you enjoy your career.

If you are a practicing Buddhist or meditate regularly, this section will cover the things you already know and practice. If you are like the rest of us, you really need to read this section carefully.

Have any of these ever happened to you?

- You are reading the news or a book but not absorbing the content because you are thinking about what is happening in the next room.
- You are watching your child's softball game, but your mind is on what you need to do tomorrow at work.
- You are at the dinner table with your spouse, but planning your morning staff meeting.
- You are on the phone with a loved one, but rather than listening, you are thinking about your shopping list.

This happens to all of us—some more than others. It is not because we love our work more than our children's softball games. It is not because we care more about shopping than our loved one's conversation. It is because we Americans are so immediate-future-oriented and activity-based that we have difficulty living in the moment and being mindful.

Psychologists Kirk Warren Brown and Richard Ryan found that mindfulness increases individuals' psychological well-being and lowers stress. They, along with other researchers, characterize mindfulness as being a higher quality of consciousness. And consciousness has two components: awareness and attention.[4] As such, being mindful, or fully present, will have the added benefits of allowing you to offer more of yourself to those you love and improving your own well-being.

The two concepts around being mindful seem straightforward enough:

- *Be aware* of the present environment.
- *Be attentive* and focus your awareness to that which matters most.

Think of the practice of mindfulness as a flashlight beam. Direct your attention light beam to the situation and then focus the beam so the intensity of the awareness shines only on whatever deserves your attention (your child stealing second base; the news story you are reading). These two concepts seem easy in theory, but tend to be difficult in practice for many people. It is human nature for our minds to wander; classroom teachers often call this "daydreaming," and it is a rare student who has never done it. Really, try practicing mindfulness. It will change your behaviors tremendously.

To make this even more difficult (sorry), being mindful and present in the nonwork spheres of your life are especially challenging for those with multiple-act careers. A stimulating career requires greater demands on cognitive capacity, and those who are attracted to exercising their cognitive muscle have a more difficult time dialing it down. But you can't be in "career mode" 24/7; there are times when you need to only be aware and attentive to the activities happening in the lives of your loved ones.

Unless you master the art of mindfulness in nonwork situations, those you love will feel as though you are not really paying attention or don't care about what is happening to them in their lives. You might feel as though you are mindful when you attend the softball game or listen to your loved one on the phone—but, if your attention is elsewhere, you are not really present. *Your loved ones deserve your full attention and, I promise, your career acts will not suffer from offering it.*

There are many books written about ways to improve mindfulness. Applying the advice to your career, I would encourage you to try (or at least start with) the following:

- **Plan to increase your mindfulness**—Make being mindful a conscious decision in the nonwork spheres of your life. For example, before dinner, think about the activity of being fully present at the dinner table. During the meal, if your attention starts to drift, try to catch yourself and bring your attention and awareness back to where you are. Be intentional about making an extra effort to do this whenever you are engaging with a loved one, even in the most mundane situations.

- **Clear the mental decks**—If there is something pressing that will keep you from focusing your attention, try to clear your mental deck before engaging with your loved ones. For example, do not return your loved one's call in the middle of the day when you know you will have many things on your mind. Instead, wait for a time when your work is at a lull and it is easier to be fully present.

- **Engage the active moments**—If you stay present in the moments requiring your interaction, you will learn more about the details of the lives of your loved ones and derive more intense emotions from the experience. Get into the habit of asking sincere and nonjudgmental questions about what your loved one is doing or discussing. For example, as you stay "in the moment" during a conversation, try not to evaluate but instead to listen and inquire out of curiosity and a desire for clarification. Asking such questions will encourage your active attention and help you to empathize more fully with your loved one.

- **Savor the passive moment**—Gurus in mindfulness encourage us to be present and savor the simplest acts of our lives: the feeling of the water in the shower, the taste of our toast in the morning, the fragrance of the garden when we arrive home. Personally, because I am not particularly sophisticated with meditation or mindfulness, I prefer to begin with some of life's bigger things. (Frankly, although I know I am frustrating every expert in mindfulness and meditation, I often get my best ideas in the shower. I am far from mindful in every situation.)

  Starting from a more basic place, savor the moments you have with your spouse or partner, children, extended family, and friends. Enjoy the experience of playing a sport or engaging in a hobby. As you practice the habit of focusing more of your attention and awareness into the experience, you will become more present.

- **Take nothing for granted**—Simple acts of kindness, compassion, and gratitude also help focus us more to the moments in all of the spheres of our lives. If you remember to say "thank you" for the simplest of things, you experience the simplest of things.

Use Exercise 19 to identify ways you can be more mindful and present across the many spheres of your life.

Exercise 19: Being Present and Mindful Across the Spheres of Your Life

Consider the following spheres of your nonwork life. Try to think of some specific ways you can be more mindful in these nonwork life spheres.

With your spouse or life partner

What are some things you can do to be more present?

1. _____
2. _____
3. _____

With your children

What are some things you can do to be more present?

1. _____
2. _____
3. _____

With your other family members

What are some things you can do to be more present?

1. _____
2. _____
3. _____

With your close friends

What are some things you can do to be more present?

1. _____
2. _____
3. _____

In your personal activities (such as hobbies or sports)

What are some things you can do to be more present?

1. _____
2. _____
3. _____

In your social activities
What are some things you can do to be more present?
1. _____
2. _____
3. _____

In other spheres of your life
What are some things you can do to be more present?
1. _____
2. _____
3. _____

Unbridled enthusiasm for your career acts is wonderful in many regards because it is energy giving and fulfilling. It is, remember, only one sphere of your life and I want you to *Get a Life*—a stimulating, fulfilling, and loving life. Multiple-act careers need to operate in concert with the other spheres of your life. You never want to leave your loved ones in the wake of a career; you want them to enjoy the ride— a great life—with you.

conclusions

"Choose a job you love, and you will never have to work a day in your life."
Confucius (551 BC–479 BC)

Satisfying career acts—*a job you love* in Confucius's words—are within your reach. Although the world has changed in the past 2,500 years, finding your career happiness is still an actively owned process. If there is only one motivational message I want you to take away from this book, it is to take personal ownership of your career. Love it or hate it—it is yours. You have choices to make; time, money, and energy to allocate; and a life to live (and harmonize). No employer, no boss or mentor, no professor or teacher, no parent or spouse—no one—will be able to create the career that is right for you; *it is your responsibility to create your own fulfilling career.*

The reality of the global economy has changed the backdrop for how your career fulfillment will likely be achieved. The proverbial rug has been pulled out from under many who thought there was a direct path from education to a fulfilling career. The secret is out: Those days are gone. (Pass it on.) With the dramatic changes to the psychological contract, please rethink whether you want to tie your destiny to the destiny of any one employer. Your ability to survive layoffs is really not an indicator of your career success unless you are truly fulfilled doing the work that you do with your employer. If you are not fulfilled, I am not asking you to leave your job. Rather, consider building a second career act. The benefit of taking control of your own career destiny and giving yourself options will be liberating.

Now, it is up to you to find your career happiness and fulfillment, whatever way you want to define it. There are no words on a page that can directly give you work-life balance, financial and professional freedom, and the opportunity to find fulfillment in all you do. It is your turn to put the ideas contained in these pages into action. Engage the same level of commitment that you would to your employer and give it to yourself.

Everyone deserves the opportunity to dream, explore, and prosper. You need to *dream* to stoke the creative energies that allow you to see what might be possible. You need to *explore* to uncover how to get there—and learn what you enjoy, how you like to work, what comes naturally, and the path to pursue that will be most fulfilling for you. *Prosperity* follows from dreaming and exploring. I know prosperity, career satisfaction, and fulfillment are well within your reach, provided you are willing to engage in the following:

- **Dream about your options for career acts and explore your possibilities**—It is not silly to give yourself the luxury of dreaming again. If you are too jaded to dream as an adult, try to remember what your childhood dreams were. There is likely some adult insight that can be gleaned from those childhood dreams. (Please watch or rewatch Randy Pausch's *Last Lecture* on YouTube.) If you are really stuck at the gate and cannot think of anything you would want to do in an ideal career act, ask a friend, a spouse, or anyone who loves you and knows you well for suggestions. These conversations are free—so are your dreams.

- **Change your relationship with your concept of work**— You work for yourself, not your résumé. Direct where you want to take your career, being honest with the values you have for work. It is perfectly fine to say that you don't want to engage many of your hours each week in a career. That is fine and great self-knowledge that you should be building career acts that involve passive income.

- **Stop following the outdated advice you were given in high school or college**—You don't need to hate what you do at the start of your career, paying your dues or doing your time so to speak. You do, however, need to consider how you will effectively gain the knowledge, skills, and abilities you will need to succeed in your career act. These two are different: Your employer controls the former, whereas you control the latter.

- **Shed outmoded beliefs that lead you to (consecutive) unfulfilling jobs**—Many are discussed in this book. The most insidious is negativity or the belief that there is no way out, you cannot enjoy what you do, and any other self-doubting things that keep you from finding your happiness. Self-doubt and negativity will always leave you with mediocrity in your career. I am not a Pollyanna and do not want you to be one either: Optimism, in the absence of a plan for building career acts, will not offer you a fulfilling career.

- **Don't stay too long in a job that is not moving you closer to an ideal career act**—*If your job is not moving you closer to the career you want, why are you staying in it?* Plan your exit. Plan how you will build your next career act. Don't make a wild leap without a safety net, but start building another career act to make your exit from your job less stressful. Do not wait too long. Assess the risk of your job accurately. Remember, you are probably staying too long in a job if your employer is financially unstable, you are not in a critical role, or your performance is less than stellar. Waiting too long and being downsized or fired forces you to scramble for another job and the cycle continues when you accept another job you don't really enjoy. Plan ahead for your moves—the jobs you take and your exits.

- **Manage your career the way you manage your investment portfolio**—Everyone has a different tolerance for risk, so each person who reads this paragraph will hear a somewhat different message. That is just fine, provided the message is heard. Some career acts (as any other financial investments) are considered a high risk, but offer an associated high reward, if successful. Other career acts grow more slowly and are considered to be steady sources of income. Think of your multiple-act career as a financial investment portfolio and mix higher-risk career acts with some slow and steady career acts in a way most comfortable for your level of risk and stage of life.

- **Protect your resources and remain true to your values**—Your time, money, energy, health, and the people who work for you are all resources affecting the advancement of your career and the success of your career acts. Protect and manage these resources well. Also, be honest with yourself on how you want to configure your finite resources to create career acts most consistent with your personal values.

I know that having a satisfying career and developing great career acts takes some serious, planned, and purposeful effort on your part. I know the ride, as you progress in your career, is not linear. I know the choices might not always lead where you had hoped and you might have some false starts along the way to creating your career acts. I know, in my heart, an exciting, balanced, rewarding, and fulfilling career is well worth it.

Please visit my Web site, www.PaulaCaligiuri.com. On this Web site, I share tips and tools to help you find the personal fulfillment and the prosperity that follows from a successful and satisfying career. In addition to this book, this Web site offers actionable advice on how to craft your career to create the stimulating, secure, and balanced work situation you desire. You are welcome to follow me on Twitter (PaulaCaligiuri) and Facebook.

I would like to hear from you. I invite you to share your multiple-act career and the steps you are taking to advance any of your career acts. You can post comments or send e-mails on the Web site, www. PaulaCaligiuri.com. Please share with me how the ideas in the book have helped you—which ones were particularly useful and any questions you might have. I'll do my best to answer your questions and address the broader issues through blog posts. A better understanding of your questions will enable me to more clearly offer relevant advice and tools on the Web site and blog.

I encourage you to share this book and Web site with those you know who are job changers, job seekers, those frustrated in their careers, current students, and new graduates. Everyone should know that the employment game has changed and they need to play a more active role in finding and creating their own happiness. Everyone deserves to have a fulfilling, stimulating, and secure career.

endnotes

Introduction

1. John J. Heldrich Center for Workforce Development from Rutgers, The State University of New Jersey. "The Anguish of Unemployment." Nationwide Work Trends Survey of 1,200 Unemployed U.S. Workers Reveals the Economic and Personal Costs of Prolonged Joblessness. September 3, 2009. http://www.heldrich.rutgers.edu/uploadedFiles/Publications/Heldrich_Anguish_of_Unemployment(2).pdf

2. Rousseau, Denise M. *Psychological Contracts in Organizations: Understanding Written and Unwritten Agreements*. Newbury Park, CA: Sage, 1996.

   Rousseau, Denise. 1989. "Psychological and implied contracts in organizations." *Employee Rights and Responsibilities Journal* 2:121–139.

3. I've worked with some of the best human resource managers on the planet, and it is my heartfelt belief that they might have the most difficult roles in organizations today; they are trying to concurrently engage and develop the workforce while competing in an increasingly more challenging global economy. I have seen, firsthand, the sadness many of the leading HR executives experience when they need to initiate layoffs for their organizations. Although they are businesspeople charged with helping their organizations compete, many of these human resource executives are also very compassionate people who find downsizing and layoffs to be emotionally devastating.

Chapter 1

1. Bureau of Labor Statistic's 2007 American Time Use Survey, providing information about the activities people do during the day and how much time they spend doing them.

2. Monster Worldwide Inc.; http://about-monster.com/content/monster-poll-shows-sunday-night-insomnia-afflicts-workers-around-globe

Chapter 2

1. McClelland, D. C., and D. H. Burnham. 1976. "Power is the great motivator." *Harvard Business Review*, 54:100–110.

   McClelland, D. C., R. Koestner, and J. Weinberger. 1989. "How do self-attributed and implicit motives differ?" *Psychological Review* 96:690–702.

   McClelland, D. C., and R. E. Boyatzis. 1982. "Leadership motive patterns and long-term success in management." *Journal of Applied Psychology* 67:737–743.

2. Schein, E. 1996. *Career Anchors, Discovering your Real Values*. Oxford: Pfeiffer.

3. The individual assessment has an associated fee.

4. This career anchor was added by Dr. Vesa Suutari and his colleagues, based on their research studies; Suutari, V., and M. Taka. 2004. "Career anchors of managers with global careers." *Journal of Management Development* 23:833–847.

5. Pausch, Randy, and Jeffry Zaslow. 2008. *The Last Lecture*. New York: Hyperion.

Chapter 3

1. Statistic cited in Liz Pulliam Weston's article for *MSN Money* titled "How much college debt is too much?" http://articles.moneycentral.msn.com/CollegeAndFamily/CutCollegeCosts/HowMuchCollegeDebtIsTooMuch.aspx accessed on August 14, 2009.

2. Posted on www.CollegeGrad.com, accessed on April 15, 2009.

3. A study conducted by the National Association of Colleges and Employers (NACE), *Job Outlook 2009 Spring Update*, released on March 4, 2009.

4. Gladwell, Malcolm. 2008. *Outliers: The Story of Success*. New York: Little, Brown and Company.

Chapter 4

1. For more information about The Flying Wallendas, see www.wallenda.com.

2. Mark Huselid, Dick Beatty, and Brian Becker have written extensively on the way organizations should manage their human resource capital. They have a series of books and articles on this topic, including "A Players:" or "A Positions:" "The Strategic Logic of Workforce Management," *Harvard Business Review*, 2005.

3. David Lepak and Scott Snell have written extensively on the topic of the human resource architecture in organizations. They have a series of books and articles on this topic, including "The human resource architecture: Toward a theory of human capital allocation and development." *Academy of Management Review*, 1999.

4. For women in particular, I like Cathie Black's book, *Basic Black: The Essential Guide for Getting Ahead at Work (and in Life)*. Crown Business Publishers, 2007.

5. I am not referring to homogeneity in terms of race, gender, age, and so on. If you are part of a minority group and truly see no minorities in senior levels of management, you will need to think through whether you believe this is really a glass ceiling (one that will keep you from moving ahead).

Chapter 5

1. Faragher, E., M. Cass, and C. L. Cooper. 2005. "The relationship between job satisfaction and health: a meta-analysis." *Occupational Environmental Medicine* 62:105–112.

2. Levine, James, and Yeager, Selene. 2009. *Move a Little, Lose a Lot: New N.E.A.T. Science Reveals How to Be Thinner, Happier, and Smarter*. New York: Crown Publishers.

3. McKnight-Eily, Lela R. 2006. "Perceived Insufficient Rest or Sleep—Four States, 2006." CDC's National Center for Chronic Disease Prevention and Health Promotion, report released in February 2008.

4. Maas, James B. 1998. *Power Sleep: The Revolutionary Program That Prepares Your Mind for Peak Performance.* New York: HarperCollins. See also www.powersleep.org/.

5. Berk, Lee. "Laughter May Indeed Be the Best Medicine: Study Shows Laughing Changes Blood Chemistry, Helps Protect Against Disease." This paper was presented at the 2006 meeting of the American Physiological Society.

6. Expedia.com—2008 International Vacation Deprivation™ Survey Results. Expedia.com has a site dedicated to this topic: www.expedia.com/vacationdeprivation.

7. The Vacation Gap, a study conducted by Air New Zealand, can be found at www.vacationgap.com/findings.

Chapter 6

1. NIOSH (1999). "Stress at work." U.S. National Institute for Occupational Safety and Health, DHHS (NIOSH) Publication Number 99-101. The American Institute of Stress has an excellent Web site and a section dedicated to job-related stress. The Web site is www.stress.org.

2. Kompier, Michiel, and Cary Cooper. 1999. *Preventing Stress, Improving Productivity: European Case Studies in the Workplace.* London: Routledge.

3. The Nielsen Company 2008 Report on television viewing.

4. See, for example: Lohr, Steve. "Slow down, brave multitasker, and don't read this in traffic." *New York Times.* March 25, 2007, p. 1.

   Strain, Jeffrey. "Why multitasking wastes time and money." *TheStreet.com,* November 14, 2007. http://www.thestreet.com/print/story/10389744.html (accessed March 2, 2009).

   Rubinstein, Joshua S., David E. Meyer, and Jeffrey E. Evans. "Executive control of cognitive processes in task switching." *Journal of Experimental Psychology – Human Perception and Performance* Vol. 27, No. 4.

5. Hembrooke, Helene, and Geri Gay. 2003. "The laptop and the lecture: the effects of multitasking in learning environments." *Journal of Computing in Higher Education* Vol. 15, No. 1.

6. Rubinstein, Joshua S., David E. Meyer, and Jeffrey E. Evans. 2001. "Executive control of cognitive processes in task switching." *Journal of Experimental Psychology—Human Perception and Performance* Vol. 27, No. 4, 763–797.

7. For more information on assessing your readiness, see "Are You Ready for a Small Business?" Source: *U.S. Small Business Administration.*

8. Giridharadas, Anand. "For tips on frugality, look to India." *International Herald Tribune*, December 18, 2008.

Chapter 7

1. Arvey, Richard, Itzhak Harpaz, and Hui Liao. 2004. "Work centrality and post-award work behavior of lottery winners." *The Journal of Psychology*, 138:5, 404–420.

2. From www.divorcerate.org.

3. The American Academy of Matrimonial Lawyers is a nonprofit association of attorneys who are experts in family law. Their publication "Making Marriage Last" is listed on their Web site at www.aaml.org/files/public/ Making_Marriage_Last.htm.

4. Brown, K. W., & Ryan, R. M. 2003. "The benefits of being present: mindfulness and its role in psychological well-being." *Journal of Personality and Social Psychology* Vol. 84, No. 4, 822–848.

**Art Center College Library
1700 Lida Street
Pasadena, CA 91103**

index

Art Center College Library
1700 Lida Street
Pasadena, CA 91103

In an increasingly competitive world, it is quality of thinking that gives an edge—an idea that opens new doors, a technique that solves a problem, or an insight that simply helps make sense of it all.

We work with leading authors in the various arenas of business and finance to bring cutting-edge thinking and best-learning practices to a global market.

It is our goal to create world-class print publications and electronic products that give readers knowledge and understanding that can then be applied, whether studying or at work.

To find out more about our business products, you can visit us at www.ftpress.com.